The Seven Words

Steven Pinker is the Johnstone Family Professor in the Department of Psychology at Harvard University. Until 2003, he taught in the Department of Brain and Cognitive Sciences at MIT. He conducts research on language and cognition, writes for publications such as the *New York Times*, *Time* and *Slate*, and is the author of six books, including *The Language Instinct*, *How the Mind Works* and *The Blank Slate*.

STEVEN PINKER

THE SEVEN WORDS YOU CAN'T SAY ON TELEVISION

PENGUIN BOOKS

PENGUIN BOOKS

Published by the Penguin Group
Penguin Books Ltd, 80 Strand, London WC2R ORL, England
Penguin Group (USA) Inc., 375 Hudson Street, New York, New York 10014, USA
Penguin Group (Canada), 90 Eglinton Avenue East, Suite 700, Toronto, Ontario,
Canada M4P 2Y3 (a division of Pearson Penguin Canada Inc.)
Penguin Ireland, 25 St Stephen's Green, Dublin 2, Ireland (a division of Penguin Books Ltd)
Penguin Group (Australia), 250 Camberwell Road, Camberwell, Victoria 3124, Australia
(a division of Pearson Australia Group Pty Ltd)
Penguin Books India Pvt Ltd, 11 Community Centre, Panchsheel Park,
New Delhi – 110 017, India
Penguin Group (NZ), 67 Apollo Drive, Rosedale, North Shore 0632, New Zealand
(a division of Pearson New Zealand Ltd)
Penguin Books (South Africa) (Pty) Ltd, 24 Sturdee Avenue, Rosebank,
Johannesburg 2196, South Africa

Penguin Books Ltd, Registered Offices: 80 Strand, London WC2R ORL, England

www.penguin.com

First published in *The Stuff of Thought* in the United States of America
by Viking Penguin 2007
First published in *The Stuff of Thought* in Great Britain by Allen Lane 2007
This extract published in Penguin Books 2008

1

Copyright © Steven Pinker, 2007
All rights reserved

The moral right of the author has been asserted

Grateful acknowledgement is made for permission to reprint excerpts from the following
copyrighted works: "This Be the Verse" from *Collected Poems* by Philip Larkin. Copyright
© 1988, 2003 by the Estate of Philip Larkin. Reprinted by permission of Farrar, Strauss and
Giroux, LLC and Faber and Faber Ltd

Printed in England by Clays Ltd, St Ives plc

978-0-141-03872-8

www.greenpenguin.co.uk

Mixed Sources
Product group from well-managed
forests and other controlled sources
www.fsc.org Cert no. SA-COC-1592
© 1996 Forest Stewardship Council
FSC

Penguin Books is committed to a sustainable future
for our business, our readers and our planet.
The book in your hands is made from paper
certified by the Forest Stewardship Council.

Freedom of speech is a foundation of democracy, because without it citizens can't share their observations on folly and injustice or collectively challenge the authority that maintains them. It's no coincidence that freedom of speech is enshrined in the first of the ten amendments to the Constitution that make up the Bill of Rights, and is given pride of place in other statements of basic freedoms such as the Universal Declaration of Human Rights and the European Convention on Human Rights.

Just as clearly, freedom of speech cannot be guaranteed in every circumstance. The U.S. Supreme Court recognizes five kinds of unprotected speech, and four of the exclusions are compatible with the rationale for enshrining free speech as a fundamental liberty. Fraud and libel are not protected, because they subvert the essence of speech that makes it worthy of protection, namely, to seek and share the truth. Also unprotected are advocacy of imminent lawless behavior and "fighting words," because they are intended to trigger behavior reflexively (as when someone shouts "Fire!" in a crowded theater) rather than to exchange ideas.

Yet the fifth category of unprotected speech— obscenity—seems to defy justification. Though some prurient words and images are protected, others cross a vague and contested boundary into the category of "obscenity," and the government is free to outlaw them. And in broadcast media, the state is granted even broader powers, and may ban sexual and scatological language that it classifies as mere "indecency." But why would a democracy sanction the use of government force to deter

I

the uttering of words for two activities—sex and excretion—that harm no one and are inescapable parts of the human condition?

In practice as well as in theory, the prosecution of obscene speech is a puzzle. Throughout history people have been tortured and killed for criticizing their leadership, and that is the fate of freethinkers in many parts of the world today. But in liberal democracies the battle for free speech has mostly been won. Every night millions of people watch talk-show hosts freely ridiculing the intelligence and honesty of the leaders of their nation. Of course, eternal vigilance is the price of liberty, and civil libertarians are rightly concerned with potential abridgments of speech such as those in copyright law, university speech codes, and the USA Patriot Act. Yet for the past century the most famous legal battles over free speech have been joined not where history would lead us to expect them—in efforts to speak truth to power—but in the use of certain words for copulation, pudenda, orifices, and effluvia. Here are some prominent cases:

- In 1921, a magazine excerpt from James Joyce's *Ulysses* was declared obscene by an American court, and the book was banned in the United States until 1933.
- D. H. Lawrence's *Lady Chatterley's Lover,* written in 1928, was not published in the United Kingdom until 1960, whereupon Penguin Books was prosecuted (unsuccessfully) under the Obscene Publications Act of 1959.

- *Lady Chatterley* was also banned from the United States, together with Henry Miller's *Tropic of Cancer* and John Cleland's *Fanny Hill*. In a series of court decisions reflecting the changing sexual mores of the 1960s, the bans were overturned, culminating in a Supreme Court ruling in 1973.

- Between 1961 and 1964, the comedian Lenny Bruce was repeatedly arrested for obscenity and banned from performing in many cities. Bruce died in 1966 while appealing a four-month sentence imposed by a New York court, and was finally pardoned by Governor George Pataki thirty-seven years after his death.

- The Pacifica Radio Network was fined in 1973 by the Federal Communications Commission for broadcasting George Carlin's monologue "Seven Words You Can Never Say on Television." The Supreme Court upheld the action, ruling that the FCC could prohibit "indecent" language during hours when children might stumble upon a broadcast.

- The FCC fined Howard Stern's popular radio program repeatedly, prompting Stern to leave broadcast radio in 2006 for the freedom of satellite radio. Many media experts predicted that it would be a tipping point in the popularity of that medium.

Other targets of sanctions include Kenneth Tynan, John Lennon, Bono, 2 Live Crew, Bernard Malamud, Eldridge

Cleaver, Kurt Vonnegut, Eric Idle, and the producers of *Hair* and *M*A*S*H*.[1]

The persecution of swearers has a long history. The third commandment states, "Thou shalt not take the name of the Lord thy God in vain," and Leviticus 24:16 spells out the consequences: "He that blasphemeth the name of the Lord shall be put to death." To be sure, the past century has expanded the arenas in which people can swear. As early as 1934, Cole Porter could pen the lyric "Good authors, too, who once knew better words / Now only use four-letter words / Writing prose. Anything goes." Most of the celebrity swearers of the twentieth century prevailed (if only posthumously), and many recent entertainers, such as Richard Pryor, Eve Ensler, and the cast of *South Park*, have cussed with impunity. Yet it's still not the case that anything goes. In 2006 George W. Bush signed into law the Broadcast Decency Enforcement Act, which increased the fines for indecent language tenfold and threatened repeat offenders with the loss of their license.

Taboo language, then, enters into a startling array of human concerns, from capital crimes in the Bible to the future of electronic media. It stakes out the frontier of free speech in liberal democracies, not only in government control of the media but in debates over hate speech, fighting words, and sexual harassment. And of course it figures in our everyday judgments of people's character and intentions.

Whether they are referred to as swearing, cursing, cussing, profanity, obscenity, indecency, vulgarity, blasphemy, expletives, oaths, or epithets; as dirty, four-letter, or taboo words; or as bad, coarse, crude, foul, salty, earthy, raunchy, or off-color language, these expressions raise many puzzles for anyone interested in language as a window into human nature. The fear and loathing are not triggered by the concepts themselves, because the organs and activities they name have hundreds of polite synonyms. Nor are they triggered by the words' sounds, since many of them have respectable homonyms in names for animals, actions, and even people. The unprintable can become printable with a hyphen or asterisk, and the unsayable sayable with the flip of a vowel or consonant. Something about the *pairing* of certain meanings and sounds has a potent effect on people's emotions.

Shakespeare wrote, "But words are words. I never yet did hear / That the bruised heart was pierced through the ear." Yet most people don't see it that way. The FCC and network censors are not inveterate prudes; they are responding to a huge constituency of listeners who light up a station switchboard like a Christmas tree when an actor or guest lets slip an obscenity. To these guardians of decency, profanity is self-evidently corrupting, especially to the young. This argument is made in spite of the fact that everyone is familiar with the words, including most children, and that no one has ever spelled out how the mere hearing of a word could corrupt one's morals.

To the libertines, what's self-evident is that linguistic taboos are absurd. A true moralist, they say, should hold that it's violence and inequality that are "obscene," not sex and excretion. And the suppression of plain speaking about sex only leads to teen pregnancy, sexually transmitted disease, and the displacement of healthy sexual energy into destructive behavior. This air of progressiveness helped to make Bruce a martyr among artists and intellectuals: "A moral conscience second to none," wrote the critic Ralph J. Gleason; "Saint Lenny, I should call him; he died for our sins," wrote the performance artist Eric Bogosian.[2]

Yet since the 1970s, some of the progressive constituencies that most admired Bruce have imposed linguistic taboos of their own. During the O. J. Simpson trial, the prosecutor Christopher Darden referred to the *n*-word as "the dirtiest, filthiest, nastiest word in the English language, and it has no place in a courtroom." Yet it has repeatedly found its way into the courtroom, most famously in the Simpson trial to prove that a police officer was a racist, and in other trials to determine whether a person can be fired for using it, or excused for assaulting someone else who uses it.[3] And in "the new Victorianism," casual allusions to sex, even without identifiable sexism, may be treated as forms of sexual harassment, as in Clarence Thomas's remarks about porn stars and pubic hair.[4] So even people who revile the usual bluenoses can become gravely offended when they hear words on their own lists of taboos.

Another puzzle about swearing is the range of topics that are the targets of taboo.[5] The seven words you can never say on television refer to sexuality and excretion: they are names for feces, urine, intercourse, the vagina, breasts, a person who engages in fellatio, and a person who acts out an Oedipal desire. But the capital crime in the Ten Commandments comes from a different subject, theology, and the taboo words in many languages refer to perdition, deities, messiahs, and their associated relics and body parts. Another semantic field that spawns taboo words across the world's languages is death and disease, and still another is disfavored classes of people such as infidels, enemies, and subordinate ethnic groups. But what could these concepts—from mammaries to messiahs to maladies to minorities—possibly have in common?

A final puzzle about swearing is the crazy range of circumstances in which we do it. There is cathartic swearing, as when we hit our thumb with a hammer or knock over a glass of beer. There are imprecations, as when we suggest a label or offer advice to someone who has cut us off in traffic. There are vulgar terms for everyday things and activities, as when Bess Truman was asked to get the president to say *fertilizer* instead of *manure* and she replied, "You have no idea how long it took me to get him to say *manure*." There are figures of speech that put obscene words to other uses, such as the barnyard epithet for insincerity, the army acronym *snafu*, and the gynecological-flagellative term for uxorial dominance. And then there are the adjective-like expletives that salt the speech and split the words of soldiers, teenagers, Australians, and others affecting a breezy speech style.

This chapter is about the puzzle of swearing—the strange shock and appeal of words like *fuck, screw,* and *come; shit, piss,* and *fart; cunt, pussy, tits, prick, cock, dick,* and *asshole; bitch, slut,* and *whore; bastard, wanker, cocksucker,* and *motherfucker; hell, damn,* and *Jesus Christ; faggot, queer,* and *dyke;* and *spick, dago, kike, wog, mick, gook, kaffir,* and *nigger.* We will explore the biological roots of swearing, the areas of experience that spawn taboo words, and the occasions on which people put them to use. Finally I will ask why these words are felt to be not just unpleasant but taboo—why merely hearing or reading them is felt to be corrupting—before offering some reflections on what we should do about swearing.

Pottymouths

As with the rest of language, swearing can be called universal, though only with qualifications.[6] Certainly the exact words and concepts considered taboo can vary across times and places. During the history of a language, we often see clean words turning and dirty words turning clean.[7] Most English speakers today would be surprised to read in a medical textbook that "in women the neck of the bladder is short, and is made fast to the cunt," yet the *Oxford English Dictionary* cites this from a fifteenth-century source. In documenting such changes the historian Geoffrey Hughes has noted, "The days when the dandelion could be called the *pissabed,* a heron could be called a *shitecrow* and the windhover could be called the *windfucker* have passed away with the exuberant phallic advertisement of the codpiece."[8] The changing fortunes of taboo words can buffet the reception of a work of literature. *Huckleberry Finn,* for example, has been the target of repeated bans in American schools because *nigger,* though never a respectful term, is far more incendiary today than it was in the time and place in which Mark Twain wrote.

Words can shed their taboos over time, too. When Eliza Doolittle chirped "Not bloody likely" at an upper-class tea in *Pygmalion,* she scandalized not only her fictional companions but the audiences who saw the play when it opened in 1914. Yet by the time it was adapted into the musical *My Fair Lady* in 1956, *bloody* had become so unexceptionable that the scriptwriters worried that the humor would be lost on the audience, and added the scene in which Eliza is taken to the Ascot races and shouts at a horse, "Move your bloomin' arse!" Many parents today are horrified when their children come home from school innocently using the verbs *suck, bite,* and *blow,* unaware of their origin as words for fellatio. But those parents probably gave just as little thought to their own use of the now-innocuous *sucker* (from *cock-sucker*), *jerk* (from *jerk off*), and *scumbag* (a condom). Progressive comedians have tried to help this process along by repeating obscenities to the point of desensitization (a process that psycholinguists call semantic satiation) or by momentarily turning into linguistics professors and calling attention to the principle of the arbitrariness of the sign. Here is an excerpt from one of Lenny Bruce's best-known routines:

> Tooooooo is a preposition. To is a preposition. Commmmmme is a verb. To is a preposition. Come is a verb. To is a preposition. Come is a

verb, the verb intransitive. To come. To come. . . . It's been like a big drum solo. To come to come, come too come too, to come to come uh uh uh uh uh um um um um um uh uh uh uh uh uh—TO COME! TO COME! TO COME! TO COME! Did you come? Did you come? Good. Did you come good? Did you come good? Did you come? Good. To. Come. To. Come—Didyoucomegood? Didyouco megooddidyoucomegood?[9]

And this is from Carlin's monologue on the "Seven Words":

Shit, Piss, Fuck, Cunt, Cocksucker, Motherfucker, and Tits, wow. Tits doesn't even belong on the list, you know. It's such a friendly sounding word. It sounds like a nickname. "Hey, Tits, come here. Tits, meet Toots, Toots, Tits, Tits, Toots." It sounds like a snack, doesn't it? Yes, I know, it is, right. But I don't mean the sexist snack, I mean, New Nabisco Tits. The new Cheese Tits, and Corn Tits and Pizza Tits, Sesame Tits, Onion Tits, Tater Tits, yeah.

Tits is now clean enough to have been left out of the Clean Airwaves Act and to be printable in "The Gray Lady," the *New York Times*. But many words stay taboo for centuries, and which words become cleaner or dirtier is as capricious as the rise and fall of *Steve*.[10]

Similar desensitization campaigns have been aimed at epithets for women and minorities, who often try to "reclaim" the words by using them conspicuously among themselves. Thus we have NWA (Niggaz With Attitude, a hip-hop group); Queer Nation, queer studies, and *Queer Eye for the Straight Guy;* Dykes on Bikes (a cycling group for lesbians) and www.classicdykes.com; and the Phunky Bitches, a "real-time community of women (and men) who are into live music, travel, and a host of other interests." I have never heard of a temple brotherhood meeting at which the attendees greet each other with "What's happenin', kike!" but in the 1970s the novelist Kinky Friedman led a country band called the Texas Jewboys, and there is a hip magazine for young Jewish readers called *Heeb.* At the same time, these terms have not been neutralized so much as flaunted as a sign of defiance and solidarity, precisely because they *are* still offensive in the language community at large. Woe betide the outsider who misunderstands this, like the Hong Kong detective played by Jackie Chan in *Rush Hour* who innocently follows the lead of his African American partner and greets the black patrons of a Los Angeles bar with "Whassup, my nigger," thereby starting a small riot.

The punch of specific words can vary even more from one language to another.[11] In Québecois French, *merde* (shit) is far milder than its English equivalent, a bit closer to *crap,* and most speakers are at best dimly aware that *con* (idiot) originally meant *cunt.* But some of the worst things you can say to someone are *Tabernac!* (tabernacle), *Calisse!* (chalice), and *Sacrement!* (sacrament). In 2006 the Catholic Church tried to reclaim these words by splashing them on billboards with their original religious definitions underneath. (One columnist sighed, "Is nothing sacred?") Religious profanity is common in other Catholic regions, as it was in England before the Reformation, when sexual and scatological terms started to take over.[12]

But despite the variation across time and space, it's safe to say that most languages, probably all, have emotionally laden words that may not be used in polite conversation. Perhaps the most extreme example is Djirbal, an Aboriginal language of Australia, in which *every* word is taboo when spoken in the presence of mothers-in-law and certain cousins. Speakers have to use an entirely different vocabulary (though the same grammar) when those relatives are around. In most other languages, the taboo words are drawn from the same short list of topics from which English and French get their curses: sex, excretion, religion, death and infirmity, and disfavored groups.[13]

Claims that profanity is lacking altogether in a particular language have to be taken with a grain of salt. It's true that in many places if you ask speakers to list their profanities, they may demur. But swearing and hypocrisy go hand in hand, to the extent that some personality questionnaires include items like "I sometimes swear" as a check for lying. In *Expletive Deleted: A Good Look at Bad Language,* the linguist Ruth Wajnryb reports:

> One of my informants, an Englishman married to a Japanese woman, asked his wife the questions I was using to elicit data about Japanese. She told him she couldn't help because she didn't know any

Japanese swear words. This she said, mind you, in wide-eyed innocence to a husband who was fully aware, as she was aware that he was, from firsthand experience of her skills in that department.[14]

A review in a periodical called *Maledicta: The International Journal of Verbal Aggression* contains an extensive list of Japanese sexual insults and vulgar terms, and the other cross-cultural surveys appearing in that journal also have a familiar ring to them.[15]

Taboo speech is part of a larger phenomenon known as word magic.[16] Though one of the foundations of linguistics is that the pairing between a sound and a meaning is arbitrary, most humans intuitively believe otherwise. They treat the name for an entity as part of its essence, so that the mere act of uttering a name is seen as a way to impinge on its referent. Incantations, spells, prayers, and curses are ways that people try to affect the world through words, and taboos and euphemisms are ways that people try *not* to affect it. Even hardheaded materialists find themselves knocking wood after mentioning a hoped-for event, or inserting *God forbid* after mentioning a feared one, perhaps for the same reason that Niels Bohr hung a horseshoe above his office door: "I hear that it works even if you don't believe in it."

The Blaspheming Brain

The ubiquity and power of swearing suggest that taboo words may tap into deep and ancient parts of the emotional brain. Words have not just a denotation but a connotation: an emotional coloring distinct from what the word literally refers to, as in *principled* versus *stubborn* and *slender* versus *scrawny*. The difference is reminiscent of the way that taboo words and their synonyms differ, such as *shit* and *feces, cunt* and *vagina,* or *fucking* and *making love.* Long ago psycholinguistics identified the three main ways in which words' connotations vary: good versus bad, weak versus strong, and active versus passive.[17] *Hero,* for example, is good, strong, and active; *coward* is bad, weak, and passive; and *traitor* is bad, weak, and active. Taboo words cluster at the very bad and very strong edges of the space, though there are surely other dimensions to connotation as well.

Are connotations and denotations stored in different parts of the brain? It's not implausible. The mammalian brain contains, among other things, the limbic system, an ancient network that regulates motivation and emotion, and the neocortex, the crinkled surface of the brain, which ballooned in human evolution and which is the seat of perception, knowledge, reason, and planning. The two systems are interconnected and work together, but it's not far-fetched to suppose that words' denotations are concentrated in the neocortex, especially in the left hemisphere, whereas their connotations are spread across connections between the neocortex and the limbic system, especially in the right hemisphere.[18]

A likely suspect within the limbic system is the amygdala, an almond-shaped organ buried at the front of the temporal lobe of the brain (one on each side), which helps invest memories with emotion.[19] A monkey whose amygdalas have been removed can learn to recognize a new shape, like a striped triangle, but has trouble learning that the shape foreshadows an unpleasant event like an electric shock. In humans the amygdala "lights up"—it shows greater metabolic activity in brain scans—when the person sees an angry face or an unpleasant word, especially a taboo word.[20] Well before psychologists could scan the working brain, they could measure the emotional jolt from a fraught word by strapping an electrode on a person's finger and measuring the change in the skin conductance caused by the sudden wave of sweat. The skin response accompanies activity in the amygdala, and like the activity recorded from the amygdala itself, it can be triggered by taboo words.[21] The emotional flavoring of words seems to be picked up in childhood: bilingual people often feel that their second language is not as piquant as their first, and their skin reacts more to hearing taboo words and reprimands in their first language than in their second.[22]

The involuntary shudder set off by hearing or reading a taboo word comes from a basic feature of the language system: understanding the meaning of a word is automatic. It's not just that we don't have earlids to shut out unwanted sounds, but that once a word is seen or heard we are incapable of treating it as a squiggle or noise but reflexively look it up in memory and respond to its meaning, including its connotation. The classic demonstration is the Stroop effect, found in every introductory psychology textbook and the topic of more than four thousand scientific papers. People are asked to look through a list of letter strings and to say aloud the color of the ink in which each one is printed. Try it with this list, saying "black," "white," or "gray" for each item in turn from left to right:

word word word **word** **word** word

It should be pretty easy. Now this is even easier:

gray white **black** white **black** gray

But this is much, much harder:

white black gray black gray **white**

The explanation is that among literate adults, reading a word is such an overlearned skill that it has become mandatory: you can't will the process "off," even when you're trying to ignore the words so you can pay attention to the ink. That's why you're helped along when the experimenters arrange the ink into a word that also names its color, and slowed down when they arrange it into a name for a different color. A similar thing happens with *spoken* words. When people have to name color patches like this:

the task becomes much harder when a voice over headphones recites a sequence of distracting color words like "black, white, gray, white, gray, black."[23]

Now, taboo words are especially effective at snatching a reader's attention. You can feel the effect yourself in a Stroop test. Try naming the color of the ink in each of these words:

cunt shit fuck tits piss asshole

The psychologist Don MacKay has done the experiment, and found that people are indeed slowed down by an involuntary boggle as soon as the eyes alight on each word.[24] The upshot is that a speaker or writer can use a taboo word to evoke an emotional response in an audience quite against their wishes.

Some companies have exploited this effect by giving their products names that are similar enough to a taboo word to grab people's attention, such as the restaurant chain called Fuddruckers, the clothing brand called FCUK (French Connection UK), and the movie called *Meet the Fokkers*. Involuntary responses to taboo words can actually shape a language over the course of its history because of a linguistic version of Gresham's Law: bad words drive good words out of circulation. People often avoid using innocent terms that they fear might be misheard as profanity. *Coney,* an old name for "rabbit" that rhymes with *honey,* dropped out of use in the late nineteenth century, probably because it sounded too much like *cunt.*[25] The same is happening to the polite senses of words like *cock, prick, pussy, booty,* and *ass* (at least in America; in Britain the rude word is still *arse*). People named *Koch, Fuchs,* and *Lipschitz* often change their surnames, as did the family of Louisa May Alcott, formerly Alcox. In 1999, an aide to the mayor of Washington, D.C., resigned after describing his budget as *niggardly* at a staff meeting. A staffer had taken umbrage, even though *niggard* is a Middle English word meaning "miser" and has nothing to do with the epithet based on *negro,* the Spanish word for black, which came into English centuries later.[26] Unfair though that may be, both to the aide and to the word, *niggardly* is doomed. So are the original senses of *queer* and *gay.*

Swearing aloud, like hearing the swear words of others, taps the deeper and older parts of the brain. Aphasia, a loss of articulate language, is typically caused by damage to the cortex and the underlying white matter along the horizontal cleft (the Sylvian fissure) in the brain's left hemisphere.[27] For almost as long as neurologists have studied aphasia, they have noticed that patients can retain the ability to swear.[28] A case study of a British aphasic recorded him as repeatedly saying "Bloody hell," "Fuck off," "Fucking fucking hell cor blimey," and "Oh you bugger." The neurologist Norman Geschwind studied an American patient whose entire left hemisphere had been surgically removed because of brain cancer. The patient couldn't name pictures, produce or understand sentences, or repeat polysyllabic words, yet in the course of a five-minute interview he said "Goddammit" seven times, and "God!" and "Shit" once apiece.[29]

The survival of swearing in aphasia suggests that taboo epithets are stored as prefabricated formulas in the right hemisphere.[30] Such formulas lie at the opposite end of a continuum from propositional speech, in which combinations of words express combinations of ideas according to grammatical rules. It's not that the right hemisphere contains a profanity module, but that its linguistic abilities are confined to memorized formulas rather than rule-governed combinations. A word is the quintessential memorized chunk, and in many people the right hemisphere has a respectable vocabulary of words, at least in comprehension. The right hemisphere also can sometimes store idiosyncratic counterparts to rule-governed forms such as irregular verbs.[31] Often it commands longer memorized formulas as well, such as song lyrics, prayers, conversation fillers like *um, boy,* and *well yes,* and sentence starters like *I think* and *You can't.*

The right hemisphere may be implicated in swearing for another reason: it is more heavily involved in emotion, especially negative emotion.[32] Yet it may not be the cerebral cortex in the right hemisphere that initiates epithets but an evolutionarily older brain structure, the basal ganglia.[33] The basal ganglia are a set of clusters of neurons buried deep in the front half of the brain. Their circuitry receives inputs from many other parts of the brain, including the amygdala and other parts of the limbic system, and loops back to the cortex, primarily the frontal lobes. One of their functions is to package sequences of movements, or sequences of reasoning steps, into chunks that are available for further combining when we're learning a skill. Another is to inhibit the execution of the actions packaged into these chunks.[34] Components of the basal ganglia inhibit one another, so damage to different parts can have opposite effects. Degeneration of one part of the basal ganglia can cause

Parkinson's disease, marked by tremors, rigidity, and difficulty initiating movement. Degeneration of another part can cause Huntington's disease, resulting in chorea or uncontrolled movements.

The basal ganglia, with their role as packagers and inhibitors of behavior, have been implicated in swearing by two trails of evidence. One is a case study of a man who suffered a stroke in the right basal ganglia, leaving him with a syndrome that is the mirror image of classic aphasia.[35] He could converse fluently in grammatical sentences, but couldn't sing familiar songs, recite well-practiced prayers and blessings, or swear—even when the beginning of a curse was given to him and he only had to complete it.

The basal ganglia have a far more famous role in swearing, thanks to a syndrome that was obscure to most people until the 1980s, when it suddenly was featured in dozens of television plots: Gilles de la Tourette Syndrome, Tourette syndrome or Tourette's for short.[36] Tourette syndrome is a poorly understood neurological condition linked to abnormalities, partly hereditary, in the basal ganglia. As any couch potato knows, its most florid symptom is a vocal tic consisting of shouted obscenities, taboo ethnic terms, and other kinds of verbal abuse.[37] This symptom is called *coprolalia* (dung speech), from a Greek root also found in *coprophilous* (living in dung), *coprophagy* (feeding on dung), and *coprolite* (fossilized dinosaur poop). In fact coprolalia occurs in only a minority of people with Tourette syndrome; the more common tics are blinks, twitches, throat-clearing sounds, and repeated words or syllables.

Coprolalia shows off the full range of taboo terms, and embraces similar meanings in different languages, suggesting that swearing really is a coherent neurobiological phenomenon. A recent literature review lists the following words from American Tourette's patients, from most to least frequent:[38]

> fuck, shit, cunt, motherfucker, prick, dick, cocksucker, nigger, cockey, bitch, pregnant-mother, bastard, tits, whore, doody, penis, queer, pussy, coitus, cock, ass, bowel movement, fangu (fuck in Italian), homosexual, screw, fag, faggot, schmuck, blow me, wop

Patients may also produce longer expressions like *Goddammit, You fucking idiot, Shit on you,* and *Fuck your fucking fucking cunt.* A list from Spanish-speaking patients includes *puta* (whore), *mierda* (shit), *cono* (cunt), *joder* (fuck), *maricon* (fag), *cojones* (balls), *hijo de puta* (son of a whore), and *hostia* (host, the wafer in a communion ceremony). A list from Japan includes *sukebe* (lecherous), *chin chin* (cock), *bakatara* (stupid), *dobusu* (ugly), *kusobaba* (shitty old woman), *chikusho* (son of a whore), and an empty space in the list discreetly identified as "female sexual parts." There has even been a report of a deaf sufferer of Tourette's who produced "fuck" and "shit" in American Sign Language.

People with Tourette's experience their outbursts not as literally involuntary but as a response to an overpowering urge, much like an irresistible itch or a mounting desire to blink or yawn. This tug-of-war between an unwanted impulse and the forces of self-control is reminiscent of one of the symptoms of obsessive-compulsive disorder (OCD) called horrific temptations—the obsessive fear that one might do something awful such as shouting "Fire!" in a crowded theater or pushing someone off a subway platform. Like Tourette's, which it often accompanies, OCD seems to involve an imbalance between the brake pedal and accelerator circuits in the basal ganglia. It suggests that one of the roles of the basal ganglia is to designate certain thoughts and desires as unthinkable—taboo—in order to keep them in check. By tagging, encapsulating, and inhibiting these thoughts, the basal ganglia solve the paradox that you have to think the unthinkable in order to know what you're not supposed to be thinking—the reason that people have trouble following the instruction "Don't think of a polar bear."[39] Ordinarily the basal ganglia can hide our bad thoughts and actions with a Don't-Go-There designation, but when they are weakened, the lockboxes and safety catches can break down, and the thoughts we tag as unthinkable or unsayable assert themselves.

In unimpaired people, the so-called executive systems of the brain (comprising the prefrontal cortex and another part of the limbic system, the anterior cingulate cortex) can monitor behavior emanating from the rest of the brain and override it in midstream. This may be the origin of the truncated profanities that we use in polite company and which serve as the strongest epithets that pass the lips of vicars and maiden aunts when they stub their toes. Every one of the standard obscenities offers a choice of bowdlerized alternatives:[40]

For *God:* egad, gad, gadzooks, golly, good grief, goodness gracious, gosh, Great Caesar's ghost, Great Scott

For *Jesus:* gee, gee whiz, gee willikers, geez, jeepers creepers, Jiminy Cricket, Judas Priest, Jumpin' Jehoshaphat

For *Christ:* crikes, crikey, criminy, cripes, crumb

For *damn:* dang, darn, dash, dear, drat, tarnation (from *eternal damnation*)

For *goddam:* consarn, dadburn, dadgum, doggone, goldarn

For *shit:* shame, sheesh, shivers, shoot, shucks, squat, sugar

For *fuck* and *fucking:* fiddlesticks, fiddledeedee, foo, fudge, fug, fuzz; effing, flaming, flipping, freaking, frigging

For *bugger:* bother, boy, brother

For *bloody:* blanking, blasted, blazing, bleeding, bleeping, blessed, blighter, blinding, blinking, blooming, blow

In *Pygmalion*, Henry Higgins is admonished by his housekeeper not to swear in Eliza's presence:

MRS. PEARCE: . . . there is a certain word I must ask you not to use. The girl has just used it herself because the bath was too hot. It begins with the same letter as *bath*. She knows no better: she learnt it at her mother's knee. But she must not hear it from your lips.

HIGGINS [*loftily*]: I cannot charge myself with having ever uttered it, Mrs. Pearce. [*She looks at him steadfastly. He adds, hiding an uneasy conscience with a judicial air*] Except perhaps in a moment of extreme and justifiable excitement.

MRS. PEARCE: Only this morning, sir, you applied it to your boots, to the butter, and to the brown bread.

HIGGINS: Oh, that! Mere alliteration, Mrs. Pearce, natural to a poet.

The devices that are natural to a poet are the source of most of the euphemisms for taboo words. Alliteration and assonance figure in the rerouted profanities in the list we just saw. Rhyme gives us *ruddy* for *bloody, son of a gun* for *son of a bitch,* and the dozens of substitutions for taboo words in Cockney slang, like *raspberry* for *fart* (from *raspberry tart*) and *Friar* for *fuck* (from *Friar Tuck*). It also led to the stereotypical French expletive *Sacre bleu!* from *Sacre Dieu.*

Poetic devices generally repeat one of the mental structures that organize words in our minds, such as onsets, rimes, and codas.[41] Phonologists have also identified structures that are more abstract than these. The syllables making up a word are attached to a skeleton that defines the word's rhythmic meter and its decomposition into morphemes.[42] When parts of a linguistic skeleton are repeated in poetry or rhetoric, we have the device called structural parallelism (as in the Twenty-third Psalm's "He maketh me to lie down in green pastures / He leadeth me beside the still waters"). In the realm of swearing, we see structural parallelism in the numerous euphemisms for *bullshit* that share only its metrical and morphological structure. Many terms for insincerity are compounds made of two stressed words, either monosyllables or trochees, with primary stress on the first one:

applesauce, balderdash, blatherskite, claptrap, codswallop, flapdoodle, hogwash, horsefeathers, humbug, moonshine, poppycock, tommyrot

Another fertile ground for terms of abuse is phonetic symbolism. Imprecations tend to use sounds that are perceived as quick and harsh.[43] They tend to be monosyllables or trochees, and contain short vowels and stop consonants, especially *k* and *g*:

fuck, cock, prick, dick, dyke, suck, schmuck, dork, punk, spick, mick, chink, kike, gook, wog, frog, fag
pecker, honky, cracker, nigger, bugger, faggot, dago, paki

(In the 1970s a friend of mine saw a bumper sticker reading NO NUKES, then an unfamiliar term, and thought it was a racist slogan!) Hughes notes, "While it may be objected, quite validly, that most swearing makes no attempt at originality, . . . certain affinities with poetry can be observed. In both fields the language used is highly charged and very metaphorical; extreme, pointed effects are created by alliteration or by playing off different registers of the word-hoard against each other, and rhythm is very important."[44]

The Semantics of Swearing:
Thoughts about Gods, Disease, Filth, and Sex

Now that we have taken a tour of the linguistic, psychological, and neurological underpinnings of swearing, can we identify a common thread in its meaning and use? The most obvious thread is strong negative emotion. Thanks to the automatic nature of speech perception, a taboo word kidnaps our attention and forces us to consider its unpleasant connotations. That makes all of us vulnerable to a mental assault whenever we are in earshot of other speakers, as if we were strapped to a chair and could be given a punch or a shock at any time. To understand swearing, then, we have to examine what kinds of thoughts are upsetting to people, and why one person might want to inflict these thoughts on another.

The historical root of swearing in English and many other languages is, oddly enough, religion.[45] We see this in the third commandment, in the popularity of *hell, damn, God,* and *Jesus Christ,* and in many of the terms for taboo language itself: *profanity* (that which is not sacred), *blasphemy* (literally "evil speech" but in practice disrespect toward a deity), and *swearing, cursing,* and *oaths,* which were originally secured by the invocation of a deity or one of his symbols, like the tabernacle, chalice, and wafer incongruously found in Catholic *maledicta.*

In English-speaking countries today, religious swearing barely raises an eyebrow. Gone with the wind are the days when people could be titillated by a character in a movie saying, "Frankly, my dear, I don't give a damn." If a character today is offended by such language, it's only to depict him as an old-fashioned prude. The defanging of religious taboo words is an obvious consequence of the secularization of Western culture. As G. K. Chesterton remarked, "Blasphemy itself could not survive religion; if anyone doubts that let him try to blaspheme Odin." To understand religious vulgarity, then, we have to put ourselves in the shoes of our linguistic ancestors, to whom God and Hell were real presences.

Swearing and oaths, in the literal sense of guarantees of one's promises, take us into the Strangelovian world of paradoxical tactics, where voluntary self-handicapping can work to one's advantage.[46] Say you need to make a promise. You may want to borrow money, and so must promise to return it. You may want someone to bear or support your child and forsake all others, and so must promise to be faithful in kind. You may want to do business with someone, and so must promise to deliver goods or services in the future in exchange for something you receive today. Why should the promisee believe you, knowing that it may be to your advantage to renege? The answer is that you can submit to a contingency that would impose a penalty on you if you did renege, ideally one so certain and severe that you would always do better to keep the promise than to back out. That way your partner no longer has to take you at your word; he can rely on your self-interest.

Nowadays we secure our promises with legal contracts that make us liable if we back out. We mortgage our house, giving the bank permission to repossess it if we fail to repay the loan. We submit to marriage laws, giving our spouses the right to alimony and a division of property if we desert or mistreat them. We post a bond, which we forfeit if we fail to come through on our obligations. But before we could count on a commercial and legal apparatus to enforce our contracts, we had to do our own self-handicapping. Children still bind their oaths by saying, "I hope to die if I tell a lie." Adults used to do the same by invoking the wrath of God, as in *May God strike me dead if I'm lying* and variations like *As God is my witness, Blow me down!, Shiver me timbers!,* and *God blind me!*—the source of the British *blimey*.[47]

Such oaths, of course, would have been more credible in an era in which people thought that God listened to their entreaties and had the power to carry them out. At the same time, every time someone reneges on an oath and is not punished by the big guy upstairs, it casts doubt on his existence, his potency, or at the very least how carefully he's paying attention. The earthly representatives of God would just as soon preserve the belief that he does listen and act in matters of importance, and so are unhappy about people diluting the brand by invoking God as the muscle behind their small-time deals. Hence the proscriptions against taking the name of the Lord in vain.

Short of literally asking God to serve as one's escrow

agent, one can sanctify one's promises in a more tactful way, by bringing God into the discussion obliquely. One can link one's credibility to appurtenances of God in which he presumably takes a continuing interest, such as his name, his symbols, his writings, and his body parts. Thus we have the phenomenon of "swearing by" and "swearing on." Even today, witnesses in American court proceedings have to swear on the Bible, as if an act of perjury undetected by the legal system would be punished by an eavesdropping and easily offended God. In earlier times Englishmen swore by gruesome reminders of the crucifixion: God's blood (*'sblood*), his nails, his wounds (hence *zounds*), his hooks (*gadzooks*), and his body (*odsbodikins*).[48] They also swore by the cross, the source of children's "Cross my heart." Perhaps the most creative was Oliver Cromwell, who wrote to the Church of Scotland, "I beseech you, in the bowels of Christ, think it possible you may be mistaken."

Even if these oaths aren't seen as literally having the power to bring down divine penalties for noncompliance, they signal a distinction between everyday assurances on minor favors and solemn pledges on weightier matters. The holiness of a religious relic is a social construction that depends on its being treated with awe and reverence by everyone in a community. This requires a collective mind control in which one doesn't look at, think about, or talk about a sacred thing casually. To bring the sacred into the discussion when making a promise is to force listeners to think about something they don't casually think about and hence to indicate that one means business. By the same token, if people swear by a sacred entity too freely, its sacredness is threatened by semantic inflation, and authorities who base their power on that sacredness will take steps to prevent that from happening. Laws against "swearing" may even have popular support, since every individual wants to keep the linguistic powder dry for occasions on which *he* wants to bind an oath, and not allow others to spoil it through overuse.

Though the invocation of blood and bowels to bind an oath may seem archaic, the psychology behind it is still with us. Even a parent without an iota of superstition would not say "I swear on the life of my child" lightly. The mere *thought* of murdering one's child for ulterior gain is not just unpleasant; it should be unthinkable if one is a true parent, and every neuron of one's brain should be programmed against it. Voluntarily thinking the thought is no small matter, and it's a kind of self-threat that can enhance the credibility of a promise. The literal unthinkability of betraying an intimate or ally is the basis of the psychology of taboo in general, and this is the mindset that is tapped in swearing on something sacred, whether it be a religious trapping or a child's life.[49] And thanks to the automatic nature of speech processing, the same sacred words that consecrate promises—the "oath binding" sense of *swearing*—may be used to attract attention, to shock, or to inflict psychic pain on a listener—the "dirty word" sense of *swearing*.

Religion also figures in the other ambiguous verb for taboo language, *cursing*. As we shall see, just about any misfortune or indignity can be wished upon someone in a curse, but Christianity has furnished execrators with a particularly disagreeable thought to inflict on their targets: the possibility that they might spend eternity in Hell. Today, *Go to hell!* and *Damn you!* are among our milder epithets, but they would have packed more of a wallop in an era in which people actually feared they might be sentenced forever to searing flames, agonizing thirst, terrifying ghouls, and blood-curdling shrieks and groans. Perhaps the closest we can come to appreciating the original impact of wishes of damnation is to imagine someone looking us in the eye and saying, "I hope you are convicted of tax fraud and sentenced to twenty years in prison. I hope your cell is hot and humid and is crawling with roaches and reeks of urine and excrement. I hope you have three vicious cellmates who beat and sodomize you every night." And so on. When we consider how brutal cursing *could* be, and how brutal it must have been when most people believed in Hell, we should be grateful that most hotheads today confine themselves to a small lexicon of hackneyed scatological and sexual imprecations that were drained of their imagery long ago.

Another semantic field that has lost its sting is disease and pestilence, as in *A plague on both your houses!* (from *Romeo and Juliet*), *A pox on you!,* and the Polish-Yiddish *Cholerya!* (cholera). In an era of sanitation and antibiotics, it's hard to appreciate the power of these allusions. It helps to visualize the "Bring out your dead!" scene in *Monty Python and the Holy Grail,* or to read in a medical textbook about the pustules, hemorrhaging, eye ulcers, diarrhea, and other grisly symptoms of these diseases. The equivalent today might be "I hope you are trapped in a fire and get third-degree burns all over your body. I hope you suffer a stroke and spend your life drooling and twisted in a wheelchair. I hope you get bone cancer and waste away in front of your loved ones." Once again, cultural critics who see swearing as a sign of the coarsening of our culture should consider how mild our curses are by the standards of history. Tellingly, there is a hint of taboo in the name of our most dreaded malady, *cancer*. It has spawned euphemisms like *the big C, malignancy, neoplasm, mitotic figure*, and one that is still seen in many obituaries, *a long illness*.

Though we no longer swear about disease, we do swear about bodily effluvia and their orifices and acts of excretion. *Shit, piss,* and *asshole* are still unspeakable on network television and unprintable in most newspapers. The *New York Times*, for example, currently identifies a bestseller by the philosopher Harry Frankfurt as *"On Bull----."* *Fart* is barely more acceptable: the *Times* will print it as part of the ageist epithet *old fart* but not as the vernacular term for flatulence. *Ass* (or *arse*), *bum, snot,* and *turd* are also on the border of respectability.

Bloody is another word that calls to mind a bodily fluid. As with many taboo terms, no one really knows where it came from, because people tend not to set down their profanities in print. That has not stood in the way of people concocting various folk etymologies. Hughes notes, "I am sure that I am not the first logophile to have been informed (on several occasions and with complete assurance) that the origin of *bloody* lies in the religious ejaculation *By our lady!*"[50] Not bloody likely, say the historians. Nor is *God's blood* the source. *Bloody* is probably another word that became taboo because it refers to an icky bodily substance, perhaps the blood that oozes from a wound, perhaps menstrual blood. Menstruation is the target of several Judeo-Christian taboos. An Orthodox Jew, for example, may not shake hands with a woman on the off chance that she is "unclean."

Some people have been puzzled about why *cunt* should be taboo. It is not just an unprintable word for the vagina but the most offensive epithet for a woman in America and a not-too-polite term for a man in Britain and the Commonwealth. One might have thought that in the male-dominated world of swearing the vagina would be revered, not reviled. After all, it has been said that no sooner does a boy come out of it than he spends the rest of his life trying to get back in. The puzzle becomes less mysterious if one imagines the connotations in an age before tampons, toilet paper, regular bathing, and antifungal drugs.

On the whole, the acceptability of taboo words is only loosely tied to the acceptability of what they refer to, but in the case of taboo terms for effluvia the correlation is fairly good. *Shit* is less acceptable than *piss,* which in turn is less acceptable than *fart,* which is less acceptable than *snot,* which is less acceptable than *spit* (which is not taboo at all). That's the same order as the acceptability of eliminating these substances from the body in public.[51]

The linguists Keith Allan and Kate Burridge tried to expand this observation by administering a Revoltingness

Questionnaire to staff and students at their Australian universities.[52] Tied for first place were feces and vomit. Menstrual blood (among men) came next, followed by urine and semen. Then, in decreasing order of revolting-ness, there was a three-way tie among flatulence, pus, and nasal mucus, followed by menstrual blood (among women), belched breath, skin parings, sweat, nail parings, breath, blood from a wound, hair clippings, breast milk, and tears. The correlation with vulgarity is far from perfect: though vomit and pus are decidedly revolting, they have no taboo terms in English. Nonetheless, the vulgar words for effluvia do cluster at the top end of the scale, including the taboo terms for semen such as *cum, spunk, gizzum, jizz,* and *cream.*

Words for effluvia are taboo in many cultures, and so are the effluvia themselves. The biologists Valerie Curtis and Adam Biran summarize the results of questionnaires given in Europe, India, and Africa: "Bodily secretions are the most widely reported elicitors of the disgust emotion. Feces appear on all of the lists, while vomit, sweat, spittle, blood, pus, and sexual fluids appear frequently."[53] Effluvia have an emotional charge that makes them figure prominently in voodoo, sorcery, and other kinds of sympathetic magic.[54] People in many cultures believe that a person can be harmed by muti-lating or casting spells on his feces, saliva, blood, nails, and hair, and that a person can be protected from harm if those substances are cursed, buried, drowned, or other-wise ostentatiously discarded. The potency of these substances in people's minds also leads them to be used in medicines or charms, often in homeopathic or purified doses. The emotion of disgust and the psychology of sympathetic magic are entwined. The psychologists Paul Rozin and April Fallon have shown that modern Westerners respect the laws of voodoo in their own disgust reactions, such as recoiling from an object if it merely looks like a disgusting substance or has been in contact with one in the past.[55] Word magic simply extends this chain of associations by one link, and gives the *words* for effluvia a dreadful power as well.

The dread of effluvia, of course, can also be modulated, as it must be in sex, medicine, nursing, and the care of animals and babies. As we shall see, this desensitization is sometimes helped along with the use of euphemisms that play down the repellence of the effluvia.

The big deal that people ordinarily make out of effluvia—both the words and the substances—has puzzled many observers. As the religion scholar A. K. Reinhart puts it, "Pus, vomit, urination, menstruation, sexual fluids, and so on [are] all substances and acts that, for some reason, many cultures tend to see as repellent and, despite their constant presence in human life, as abnormal."[56] Curtis and Biran identify the reason.[57] It can't be a coincidence, they note, that the most disgusting substances are also the most dangerous vectors for disease. Feces are a route of transmission for the viruses, bacteria, and protozoans that cause at least twenty intestinal diseases, as well as ascariasis, hepatitis A and E, polio, amoebiasis, hookworm, pinworm, whipworm, cholera, and tetanus. Blood, vomit, mucus, pus, and sexual fluids are also attractive to pathogens as vehicles for getting from one body into another. In modern countries, flush toilets and garbage removal quickly separate us from our effluvia, but in the rest of the world they transmit millions of cases of disease every year. Even citizens of industrial countries may be quickly threatened with cholera and typhoid in times of war or natural disasters, such as the flooding in New Orleans in the wake of Hurricane Katrina in 2005.

The strongest component of the disgust reaction is a desire not to eat or touch the offending substance.[58] But it's also disgusting to *think* about effluvia, together with the body parts and activities that excrete them, and because of the involuntariness of speech perception, it's unpleasant to hear the words for them. The effluvia that evoke the strongest disgust reaction are viscous ones, but urine is also mildly disgusting, and the word *piss* is mildly taboo. Urine is not generally infectious, but it is, of course, a waste product that carries away metabolites and toxins that the body doesn't want, and thus it should not be appealing. Vermin make up a major class of disease vectors, and are widely considered disgusting.[59] Not surprisingly, they lend their names in English to verbal imprecations such as *rat, louse, worm, cockroach, insect,* and *slug,* though the words don't rise to the level of taboo. Why some of the words for unpleasant things are taboo in a particular culture and era, while others are not, is something of a mystery. Perhaps taboo terms have to be acquired in emotion-tinged settings in childhood. Or perhaps they are self-perpetuating, and remain taboo for as long as people treat them as taboo.

*

The other major source of taboo words is sexuality. Since the 1960s, many progressive thinkers have found these taboos to be utterly risible. Sex is a source of mutual pleasure, they reason, and should be cleansed of stigma and shame. Prudery about sexual language could only be a superstition, an anachronism, perhaps a product of spite, as in H. L. Mencken's definition of *puritanism* as "the haunting fear that someone, somewhere may be happy." Lenny Bruce ended his "Did you come?" routine by saying, "If anyone in this room finds that verb intransitive, *to come*, obscene, vile, vulgar—if it's really a hang-up to hear it and you think I'm the rankest for saying it—*you* probably can't come."

Bruce was also puzzled by our most common sexual imprecation:

> What's the worst thing you can say to anybody? "Fuck you, Mister." It's really weird, because if I really wanted to hurt you I should say "Unfuck you, Mister." Because "Fuck you" is really *nice*! "Hello, Ma, it's me. Yeah, I just got back. Aw, fuck you, Ma! Sure, I mean it. Is Pop there? Aw, fuck you, Pop!"[60]

Part of the puzzlement comes from the strange syntax of *Fuck you*, which, as we shall see, does not in fact mean "Have sex." But it also comes from a modern myopia (particularly in young men) for how incendiary sexuality can be in the full sweep of human experience.

Consider two consenting adults who have just had sex. Has everyone had fun? Not necessarily. One partner might see the act as the beginning of a lifelong relation-ship, the other as a one-night stand. One may be infecting the other with a disease. A baby may have been conceived, whose welfare was not planned for in the heat of passion. If the couple is related, the baby may inherit two copies of a deleterious recessive gene and be susceptible to a genetic defect. There may be romantic rivals in the wings who would be enraged with jealousy if they found out, or a cuckolded husband in danger of raising another man's child, or a two-timed wife in danger of losing support for her own children. Parents may have marriage plans for one of the participants, involving large sums of money or an important alliance with another clan. And on other occasions the partici-pants may not both be adults, or may not both be consenting.

Sex has high stakes, including exploitation, disease, illegitimacy, incest, jealousy, spousal abuse, cuckoldry, desertion, feuding, child abuse, and rape. These hazards have been around for a long time and have left their mark on our customs and our emotions. Thoughts about sex are likely to be fraught, and not entertained lightly. *Words* for sex can be even touchier, because they not only evoke the charged thoughts but implicate a sharing of those thoughts between two people. The thoughts, moreover, are shared "on the record," each party knowing that the other knows that he or she has been thinking about the sex under discussion, which embroils the dialogue in an extra layer of intrigue.

Evolutionary psychology has laid out the conflicts of interest that are inherent to human sexuality, and some of these conflicts play themselves out in the linguistic arena.[61] Plain speaking about sex conveys an attitude that sex is a casual matter, like tennis or philately, and so it may seem to the partners at the time. But the long-term implications may be more keenly felt by a wider circle of interested parties. Parents and other senior kin may be concerned with the thwarting of their own plans for the family lineage, and the community may take an interest in the illegitimate children appearing in their midst, and in the posturing and competition, sometimes violent, that can accompany sexual freedom. The ideal of sex as a sacred communion between a monogamous couple may be old-fashioned and even unrealistic, but it sure is convenient for the elders of a family and a society. It's not surprising to find tensions between individuals and guardians of the community over casual talk about sex (accompanied by hypocrisy among the guardians when it comes to their own casual sex).

Even keener than the sexual conflicts between young and old and between individual and society is the conflict between men and women. We are mammals, and have inherited the asymmetry that runs through that class: in every act of reproduction, females are committed to long stretches of pregnancy and lactation, while males can get away with a few minutes of copulation. A male can have more progeny if he mates with many females, whereas a female will not have more progeny if she mates with many males—though her offspring will do better if she has chosen a mate who is willing to invest in them or can endow them with good genes. Not surprisingly, in all cultures men pursue sex more eagerly,

are more willing to have casual sex, and are more likely
to seduce, deceive, or coerce to get sex.[62] All things being
equal, casual sex works to the advantage of men, both
genetically and emotionally. We might expect casual *talk*
about sex to show the same asymmetry, and so it does.
Men swear more, on average, and many taboo sexual
terms are felt to be especially demeaning to women—
hence the old prohibition of swearing "in mixed
company."[63]

A male-female difference in tolerance for sexual
language may call to mind the stereotype in which a
Victorian woman who heard a coarse remark would
raise her wrist to her forehead and swoon onto the
fainting couch. But an unanticipated consequence of the
second wave of feminism in the 1970s was a revived
sense of offense at swearing, the linguistic companion
to the campaign against pornography. Groucho Marx
might be surprised to learn that today's universities and
businesses have implemented his platform for running
Freedonia in *Duck Soup:* No one's allowed to smoke, or
tell a dirty joke. Many published guidelines on sexual
harassment include "telling sexual jokes" in their definitions, and in 1993 the veteran *Boston Globe* journalist
David Nyhan was forced to apologize and to donate
$1,250 to a women's organization when a female staffer
overheard him in the newsroom using the word
pussy-whipped with a male colleague who declined his
invitation to play basketball after work.[64] The feminist
writer Andrea Dworkin, famous for her activism against
pornography and her suggestion that all intercourse is

rape, explicitly connected coarse sexual language to the oppression of women:

> Fucking requires that the male act on one who has less power and this valuation is so deep, so completely implicit in the act, that the one who is fucked is stigmatized. . . . In the male system, sex is the penis, the penis is sexual power, its use in fucking is manhood.[65]

While it's tempting to ridicule the backlash against sexual swearing as a throwback to Victorian daintiness, it remains true that an atmosphere of licentiousness may be less conducive to women's interests than to men's. In the decade between the sexual revolution of the early 1960s and the feminist revolution of the early 1970s, many works of popular culture celebrated the overthrow of puritanism with sympathetic portrayals of lascivious men (examples include works by Joe Orton, Tom Lehrer, Woody Allen, and the Rolling Stones, the James Bond movies, and *Rowan and Martin's Laugh-In*). Revisiting these works can make for painful watching and listening. Their exuberant leering, thought to be sophisticated and risqué at the time, seems misogynistic today, with depictions of women as bimbos and an amused tolerance of rape, harassment, and spousal abuse. (A song from the musical *Hair* began, "Sodomy, fellatio, cunnilingus, pederasty. Father, why do these words sound so nasty?"—showing an indulgence toward pedophilia that would be unthinkable today.) The brief glorification of lechery in middle-class culture, bookended at one end by a challenge of youth to age and the individual to society, and at the other by a challenge of women to men, exposes some of the conflicts of interest that charge the language of sex.

Though people are seeing, talking about, and having sex more readily today than they did in the past, the topic is still not free of taboo. Most people still don't copulate in public, swap spouses at the end of a dinner party, have sex with their siblings and children, or openly trade favors for sex. Even after the sexual revolution, we have a long way to go before "exploring our sexuality" to the fullest, and that means that people still set up barriers in their minds to block certain trains of thought. The language of sex can tug at those barriers.

Five Ways to Cuss

Now that we have visited the content of taboo language (its semantics), we can turn to the ways in which it is used (its pragmatics). Recall that the common denominator of the content of swearing is an emotional charge that people would rather not have running through their minds at the drop of a hat—a sense of awe (for God and his trappings), fear (for Hell and disease), disgust (for bodily effluvia), hatred (for traitors, heretics, and minorities), or depravity (for sexuality). Because speech perception is automatic, uttering a taboo word can force a listener's mind to go in a direction it ordinarily prevents itself from going in. This helps us to focus the question of how profanity is used. Why do speakers try to impose their wills on their listeners' minds in this way? There is no single answer, because people swear in at least five different ways: descriptively (*Let's fuck*), idiomatically (*It's fucked up*), abusively (*Fuck you, motherfucker!*), emphatically (*This is fucking amazing*), and cathartically (*Fuck!!!*). Let's look at each in turn.

Many of the puzzles around profanity come down to a single question: what is it about a taboo word that makes it different from a genteel synonym that refers to the same thing? What are people responding to so strongly, for example, when they choose *feces* over *shit*, *penis* over *prick*, *vagina* over *cunt*, *have sex* over *fuck*?

The major difference is that the taboo term is dysphemistic—it calls to mind the most disagreeable aspects of the referent, rather than just pointing to it. Now, people don't like to think about feces any more than they like to see it, smell it, or touch it. Yet we are incarnate beings, for whom feces is part of life, and there are occasions on which we have no choice but to confer on what to do with it. The solution is to divide the linguistic labor between euphemisms, which refer to an entity without evoking the unwanted emotions, and dysphemisms, including taboo words, for those rhetorical occasions on which we want to rub in how truly awful the entity is.

Euphemisms and dysphemisms for taboo concepts materialize and turn over rapidly. Allan and Burridge estimate that English has accumulated more than eight hundred expressions for copulation, a thousand for a penis, twelve hundred for a vagina, and two thousand for a wanton woman (making you wonder why people make so much of a fuss about the number of Eskimo words for snow).[66] In contemporary English we find several dozen specialized terms for feces, presumably because it is both so disgusting and so unavoidable:

taboo: *shit*
mildly dysphemistic: *crap, turd*
mildly euphemistic: *waste, fecal matter, filth, muck*
formal: *feces, excrement, excreta, defecation, ordure*
with children: *poop, poo, poo-poo, doo-doo, doody, ka-ka, job, business, Number 2, BM*
of diapers: *soil, dirt, load*
medical: *stool, bowel movement*
animal, large units: *pats, chips, pies*
animal, small units: *droppings*
animal, scientific: *scat, coprolites, dung*
animal, agricultural: *manure, guano*
human, agricultural: *night soil, humanure, biosolids*

Most of the polite terms are specific to a context in which feces must be discussed and to the actions that are appropriate in that context (spreading it as fertilizer, changing a diaper, analyzing it for medical or scientific purposes, and so on). Using the euphemism thus leaves no doubt as to why a conversant is bringing up the subject.

When it comes to the referents of taboo terms, the English language has gone overboard with specialization, and fails to provide us with neutral terms for casual conversation. Even people who swear only in moments of extreme and justifiable excitement would sound rather stuffy if in conversation with a friend they used *feces*, *flatulence,* or *anus* rather than their taboo alternatives. And the words *penis* and *vagina* force us to speak in Latin, whereas our other body parts have concise Anglo-Saxon roots, in keeping with the rest of our casual vocabulary. As C. S. Lewis put it, "As soon as you deal with [sex] explicitly, you are forced to choose between the language of the nursery, the gutter, and the anatomy class."[67]

There are times, of course, when we want to remind our listeners of the disagreeable aspects of something, and that is when we turn to the language of the gutter. Sometimes for the sake of narrative vividness, sometimes out of anger, we use taboo words to convey just how vile something is:

> So the plumber wanted to talk to me while he
> was working under the sink, and I had to look
> at the crack in his ass the whole time.
> His motto in life is: If it moves, fuck it; if it
> doesn't, stab it.
> Will you pick up your dog's shit, and stop him
> from pissing on my roses!
> Then John showed me the album, and I'm
> supposed to say, "Oh, that's nice," as if his
> dick weren't hanging out there [Ringo Starr,
> describing his reaction to being shown the
> *Two Virgins* album cover, on which Lennon
> and Yoko Ono had posed nude].

Try replacing the taboo terms in these sentences with their polite synonyms (*buttocks, having sex,* and so on). They lack a certain something, because the emotional force of the speaker's reaction is no longer being conveyed. And because taboo words evoke carnal details in the minds of listeners and readers, they are often put to use in pornography and in the formula for sexual arousal requested by many consenting adults: "Talk dirty to me."

Needless to say, not everyone reserves taboo words for special rhetorical effect. The expressions "to swear like a sailor," "to cuss like a stevedore," and "locker-room language" point to the fact that swearing is the language of choice in many male-dominated and working-class circles. One reason is that swearing, which forces a listener to think about disagreeable things, is mildly aggressive, so it fits with the other trappings that men in rough-and-tumble settings brandish to advertise that they can inflict and endure pain (heavy boots, metal studs, exposed muscles, and so on). The other reason is that a conspicuous willingness to break taboos conveys an atmosphere of informality, a freedom from having to watch what you say. Of course swearing has expanded in recent decades to women and the middle class. (When I was a teenager during the heyday of the "generation gap," the father of one of my friends used to say to her, "Nancy, your mouth is like a toilet.") The trend was part of a larger development in the twentieth century toward informality, egalitarianism, and the spread of macho and cool-pose styles.

The ability of taboo words to evoke an emotional reaction is useful not just when speakers wish to convey their own distress to a listener but also when they want to create that distress in a listener from scratch. Hence we have the use of profanity in insults, execrations, and other forms of verbal abuse.

There are moments in everyone's life when one feels the urge to intimidate, punish, or downgrade the reputational stock of some other person. The crafting of maledicta has probably exercised people's language instinct more vigorously than all the other kinds of speech acts put together, and in many cultures it has been raised to a high art, sometimes called flyting. For example, there are Shakespearean insults:

PRINCE HENRY: . . . this sanguine coward, this bed-presser, this horseback-breaker, this huge hill of flesh,—

FALSTAFF: 'Sblood, you starveling, you elf-skin, you dried neat's tongue, you bull's pizzle, you stock-fish! O for breath to utter what is like thee! you tailor's-yard, you sheath, you bowcase; you vile standing-tuck,—

And Yiddish curses:

She should have stones and not children.
May all your teeth fall out but one, so you can have a toothache.
He should give it all away to doctors.

And the African American tradition known as sounding, snapping, signifying, ranking, and the dozens:

You're so ugly, when you were born the doctor
   looked at your face and looked at your ass
   and said, "It's twins."
Your mama's like a bowling ball—she gets
   picked up, fingered, thrown in the gutter, and
   then comes back for more.
Your mama's so dumb she thinks Moby Dick is
   a venereal disease.

When crafting a curse, the availability of words that trigger unpleasant thoughts in a listener or bystander is a weapon that is too handy to forbear, and so taboo words figure prominently in imprecations. People or their parts may be likened to effluvia and their associated organs and accessories (*piece of shit, asshole, cunt, twat, prick, schmuck, putz, old fart, shithead, dickhead, asswipe, scumbag, douchebag*). They can be accused of engaging in undignified sexual activities such as incest (*motherfucker*), sodomy (*bugger, sod*), fellatio (*cocksucker; You suck! You bite! You blow!*), and masturbation (*wanker, jerk*). They can be advised to undertake degrading activities (*Kiss my ass, Eat shit, Fuck yourself, Shove it up your ass*, and—my favorite—*Kiss the cunt of a cow*, from 1585).[68] They can be threatened with violence accompanied by degradation, as in *I'll stick a pig's leg up your cunt until your back teeth rattle* (from Japan), and *I'll rip your head off and shit down your windpipe*, which I overheard at a Boston bus stop. Surveys of maledicta in other languages uncover similar themes.[69] And then there is the most common obscene curse in English,

Fuck you, but to understand it we must take a closer look at taboo terms for sex.

Verbs for sex show a curious pattern. The anthropologist Ashley Montagu referred to *fuck* as "a transitive verb for the most transitive of human actions," and therein lies a tale.[70] Think of the transitive verbs for sex—the ones that fit in the slot *John verbed Mary:*

> fuck, screw, hump, ball, dick, bonk, bang, shag, pork, shtup

They're not very nice, are they? The verbs are jocular or disrespectful at best and offensive at worst. So what are the verbs that we do use in polite company when referring to the act of love?

> have sex, make love, sleep together, go to bed, have relations, have intercourse, be intimate, mate, copulate

They are *intransitive,* every one of them. The word for the sexual partner is always introduced by a preposition: have sex *with,* make love *to,* and so on. Indeed, most of them aren't even verbs of their own, but idioms that join a noun or an adjective to an insubstantial "light verb" like *have, be,* or *make.* (In *Crazy English,* Richard Lederer asks: "*To sleep with someone.* So who's sleeping? *A one-night stand.* Who's standing?") In the last section we saw many cases where a sense of decorum mandates the choice of a word. But why should it mandate something as abstruse as a grammatical construction?

Every construction chooses its verbs from a set of microclasses, each with a meaning that is conceptually compatible with the construction, if only metaphorically. Using this principle, can we discover anything about human sexuality from the syntax of the verbs for sex— the "copulative verbs," in a sense very different from the one in traditional grammar?

The polite idioms have a number of telltale grammatical traits. By lacking a distinctive verb root, they fail to specify an action with a characteristic manner of motion or kind of effect. By lacking a direct object, they specify no entity that is impinged upon or caused to change. Moreover, they are semantically symmetrical: if John had sex with Mary, it implies that Mary had sex with John, and vice versa. And all of them alternate with another intransitive construction in which the partner is not mentioned in a prepositional object but rather is part of a plural subject: *John and Mary had sex, John and Mary made love, John and Mary were intimate,* and so on. The semantics of the *non*-sexual verbs that behave in this way implies joint voluntary action, like *dance, talk, trade,* and *work: John danced with Mary, John and Mary danced,* and so on. So in the mental model presupposed by the polite verbs for sex, sex is an activity, manner unspecified, that two people jointly engage in.

Compare the ruder, transitive verbs for sex. Transitive verbs describe an agent that deliberately carries out an action that impinges on an entity, or affects the entity, or both. Though *fuck* doesn't fall perfectly into any of the five classes of transitive verbs, it does have affinities with the microclass of verbs of motion-contact-effect.[71] It can be accepted into the conative, possessor-raising, and middle constructions, but not into the contact-locative or anticausative construction. (A sense of propriety, or what's left of it, compels me to put the examples in an endnote.)[72] This is consistent with the verb's etymology from an Old Norse word for beating, striking, or thrusting, and with the fact that its transitive synonyms include *bang* and *bonk*. (The Yinglish *shtup* comes from a different metaphor: the verb in Yiddish means "to stuff.")

In a well-known paper, the linguist Quang Fuc Dong notes that *fuck* occurs far more often with a male subject than a female one, and that some speakers use the verb only with a male subject.[73] To be more exact, its semantic requirement is that the subject be the active party. In sexual encounters between two men, he notes, *Boris fucked Lionel* is grammatical if Boris is on top, and in encounters between two women *Cynthia fucked Gwendolyn* is grammatical if Cynthia used a dildo. The object of the verb, on the other hand, does not have to be female, or human, or even animate. In a memorable passage in Philip Roth's *Portnoy's Complaint,* the narrator confesses to an event that took place when he was a teenager and had discovered a piece of raw liver in the refrigerator: "Now you know the worst thing I have ever done. I fucked my own family's dinner."

If the transitive verbs for sex imply that the direct object is affected, exactly how must it be affected? The answer may be found in a Lakoffian analysis of the way that the verbs for sex take part in conceptual metaphors. Many of the transitive verbs for sex can be used metaphorically to refer to exploitation, as in the joke we used to tell about why the Québec government planned to change the provincial symbol from the fleur-de-lys to a condom: It prevents conception, allows inflation, protects a bunch of pricks, and gives you a false sense of security when you're being screwed. Metaphors in this family include *I was screwed, They fucked me over, We got shafted, I was reamed,* and *Stop dicking me around.*

The other metaphorical topic of the transitive verbs for sex is grievous damage, as in *fucked up, screwed up, buggered up,* and the British *bollixed* and *cockup.* World War II army slang included the acronyms *snafu* (Situation Normal, All Fucked Up), *tarfu* (Things Are Really Fucked Up), and *fubar* (Fucked Up Beyond All Recognition). The terms were absorbed into the argot of engineers, and today when computer programmers create a temporary file or teach a novice how to name one, they use the filename foo.bar—a bit of nerd humor. The metaphors underlying the transitive verbs for sex, then, are TO HAVE SEX IS TO EXPLOIT SOMEONE and TO HAVE SEX IS TO DAMAGE SOMEONE.

These conceptual metaphors are found in many other languages, too. In Brazilian Portuguese, the vulgar equivalent of *fuck* is *comer,* "to eat," with the man (or active homosexual partner) as the subject. This would be mysterious if the verb were a metaphor based on the mechanics of copulation, because it should be the woman's body that metaphorically eats the man's. But it fits the understanding of sex in which a woman is enjoyed and exploited by the man.

So the syntax of the verbs of sex uncovers two very different mental models of sexuality. The first is reminiscent of sex-education curricula, marriage manuals, and other sanctioned views: Sex is a joint activity, details unspecified, which is mutually engaged in by two equal partners. The second is a darker view, somewhere between mammalian sociobiology and Dworkin-style feminism: Sex is a forceful act, instigated by an active male and impinging on a passive female, exploiting her or damaging her. Both models capture human sexuality in its full range of manifestations, and if language is our guide, the first model is approved for public discourse, while the second is taboo, though widely recognized in private.

As I've mentioned, the dividing line between terms that are merely dysphemistic and those that cross over to taboo is mysterious. For many people, *excrement* has a far more unpleasant connotation than *shit*, because *excrement* is reserved for descriptions of filth and squalor whereas *shit* is used in a wider range of idioms and casual contexts. Nonetheless, *shit* is less acceptable than *excrement*. Similarly, the behavior labeled by *fuck* is nowhere near as upsetting as the behavior labeled by *rape*, yet *rape* is not a taboo word. People treat an unpleasant word as taboo to the extent that everyone else treats it as taboo, so the status of the words may be at the mercy of the boom-and-bust epidemiology that sets the fate of words and names in general.

What this all entails is that taboo words, though evocative of the nastier aspects of their referents, don't get their punch from those connotations alone. Taboo status *itself* gives a word an emotional zing, regardless of its actual referent. This gives rise to the countless idioms that incorporate taboo terms. Some of them, like *bullshit, They fucked me over, He pissed on my proposal,* and *She pissed away her inheritance,* are clearly metaphorical, projecting one of the unpleasant aspects of their vehicle onto an aspect of their topic. But a much larger number show no discernible analogy to their subject matter, and incorporate the taboo word only for its ability to pique the listener's interest:

He went through a lot of shit. Tough shit! We're up shit's creek. We're shit out of luck. A shit-load of money. Shit oh dear! [New Zealand]. Shit, eh? [New Zealand]. Let's shoot the shit. Let's smoke some shit. Put your shit over there. A lot of fancy shit. He doesn't know shit. He can't write for shit. Get your shit together. Are you shitting me? He thinks he's hot shit. No shit! All that shit. A shit-eating grin. Shitfaced [drunk]. Apeshit. Diddly-shit. Sure as shit.

It's piss-poor. Piss off! I'm pissed at him. He's pissed off. He's pissed [drunk]. Full of piss and vinegar. They took the piss out of him [British].

My ass! Get your ass in gear. Ass-backwards. Dumb-ass. Your ass is grass. Kiss your ass

goodbye. Get your ass over here. That's one
big-ass car! Ass-out [broke]. You bet your ass!
A pain in the ass.

Don't get your tits in a tangle [New Zealand].
My supervisor has been getting on my tits
[British].

Fuckin-A! Aw, fuck it! Sweet fuck-all. He's a
dumb fuck. Stop fucking around. He's such a
fuckwit [New Zealand]. This place is a real
clusterfuck ["disorganized situation," army].
Fuck a duck! That's a real mindfucker. Fuck
this shit.

More than 250 entries of this sort may be found in a
specialized dictionary by the lexicographer Jesse
Sheidlower called *The F-Word*.[74] Metaphors and idioms
can congeal into formulas that people no longer analyze.
This seems to have happened, at least in part, with the
vulgar idioms, and together with expletives like *fucking
amazing* they are the least offensive way to use taboo
words.

The affective clout of taboo words can make them
into strange synonyms: they substitute for one another
in idioms even when they have no affinity in syntax or
meaning. Many bafflingly ungrammatical profanities
must have originated in more intelligible *religious* profanities during the transition from religious to sexual and
scatological swearing in English-speaking countries:

Who (in) the hell are you? → Who the fuck are
you? (Also: Where the fuck are you going?

What the fuck are you doing? Get the fuck
out of here, etc.)
I don't give a damn → I don't give a fuck; I
don't give a shit; I don't give a sod.
Holy Mary! → Holy shit! Holy fuck!
For God's sake → For fuck's sake; For shit's
sake.

When it comes to the family ties among taboo words, then, connotation is a stronger filament than meaning or syntax. That helps explain the two great mysteries in the syntax of English profanity: what the word *fuck* is doing in *Close the fucking door,* and what it is doing in *Fuck you!*

The mysteries were first explored in what must be the strangest festschrift in the history of academia, *Studies Out in Left Field: Defamatory Essays Presented to James D. McCawley on the Occasion of His 33rd or 34th Birthday.* The late linguist Jim McCawley was one of the founders, together with George Lakoff and Haj Ross, of the school of linguistics called Generative Semantics. His contributions included a guide to the fractious field called *Thirty Million Theories of Grammar,* a primer called *Everything That Linguists Have Always Wanted to Know about Logic (But Were Ashamed to Ask),* and *The Eater's Guide to Chinese Characters,* a tutorial that empowers readers to order from the Chinese side of the menu and get the really good dishes that the Chinese patrons are always eating. Among the many unconventional aspects of this 1971 festschrift is that several of the contributions were penned by McCawley himself under the pseudonyms Quang Fuc Dong and Yuck Foo, both of the "South Hanoi Institute of Technology" (get it?). Despite the sometimes sophomoric humor and tasteless examples, the papers are sophisticated analyses of the grammar of English taboo expressions, and are still cited in scholarly work today (sometimes as "Quang (1971)" or "Dong, Q. F.").

Expletives like *bloody* and *fucking* are probably the most commonly used taboo words in casual speech, despite their nonsensical semantics and syntax. A century-old British slang dictionary includes the following in its entry for *bloody*: "Most frequently . . . as it falls with wearisome reiteration every two or three syllables from the mouths of London roughs of the lowest type; no special meaning, much less a sanguinary one, can be attached to its use."[76] Similar observations have been made about the dialect called Fuck Patois, like the story about the soldier who said, "I come home to my fucking house after three fucking years in the fucking war, and what do I fucking-well find? My wife in bed, engaging in illicit sexual relations with a male!"

The grammar of *fucking* in its expletive role made the news in 2003 when NBC broadcasted the Golden Globe Awards and Bono said, "This is really, really, fucking brilliant" on the air. The FCC originally chose not to sanction the network because their guidelines define "indecency" as "material that describes or depicts sexual or excretory organs or activities," and Bono had used the word as "an adjective or expletive to emphasize an exclamation." Cultural conservatives were outraged, and California Representative Doug Ose tried to close the loophole with the filthiest piece of legislation ever considered by Congress, the Clean Airwaves Act:

A BILL

To amend section 1464 of title 18, United States Code, to provide for the punishment of certain profane broadcasts, and for other purposes.

Be it enacted by the Senate and House of Representatives of the United States of America in Congress assembled, That section 1464 of title 18, United States Code, is amended—

(1) by inserting '(a)' before 'Whoever'; and
(2) by adding at the end the following: '(b) As used in this section, the term 'profane', used with respect to language, includes the words 'shit', 'piss', 'fuck', 'cunt', 'asshole', and the phrases 'cock sucker', 'mother fucker', and 'ass hole', compound use (including hyphenated compounds) of such words and phrases with each other or with other words or phrases, and other grammatical forms of such words and phrases (including verb, adjective, gerund, participle, and infinitive forms).

Unfortunately for Rep. Ose, the bill would not have closed the loophole after all, because it fails to specify the syntax of Bono's expletive properly (to say nothing of its misspelling of *cocksucker, motherfucker,* and *asshole,* or its misidentifying them as "phrases").

The Clean Airwaves Act assumes that *fucking* is a

participial adjective. But this is not correct. As Quang notes, with a true adjective like *lazy*, you can alternate between *Drown the lazy cat* and *Drown the cat which is lazy*.[77] But *Drown the fucking cat* is certainly not interchangeable with *Drown the cat which is fucking*. (Likewise, *Drown the bloody cat* does not mean the same thing as *Drown the cat which is bloody*.) Nor can you say *The cat seemed fucking*, *How fucking was the cat?*, or *the very fucking cat*, three more tests for adjectivehood.[78]

Some critics have poked fun at the Clean Airwaves Act for another bit of grammatical illiteracy. If anything, the *fucking* in *fucking brilliant* should be an adverb, because it modifies an adjective, and only adverbs can do that, as in *truly bad*, *very nice*, and *really big*. Yet "adverb" is the one grammatical category that Ose forgot to include in his list! As it happens, taboo expletives aren't genuine adverbs, either. Another "study out in left field" notes that while you can say *That's too fucking bad* and *That's no bloody good*, you can't say *That's too very bad* or *That's no really good*.[79] Also, as the linguist Geoffrey Nunberg has pointed out, while you can imagine the dialogue *How brilliant was it? Very*, you would never hear the dialogue *How brilliant was it? Fucking*.[80]

Most anarchically of all, expletives can appear in the middle of a word or compound, as in *in-fucking-credible*, *hot fucking dog*, *Rip van Fucking Winkel*, *cappu-fucking-ccino*, and *Christ al-fucking-mighty*—the only known case in English of the morphological process known as infixation. *Bloody* also may be infixed, as in *abso-bloody-lutely* and *fan-bloody-tastic*. In his memoir *Portrait of the Artist as a Young Dog,* Dylan Thomas writes, "You can always tell a cuckoo from Bridge End . . . it goes cuck-BLOODY-OO, cuck-BLOODY-OO, cuck-BLOODY-OO."

The semantics of expletives are as strange as their syntax. *Bloody* and *fucking* generally express disapproval, yet the disapproval is not necessarily directed at the modified noun:

INTERVIEWER: Why is British food so bad?
JOHN CLEESE: Because we had a bloody empire to run, you see?[81]

Cleese was not casting aspersions on the empire on which the sun never set; he was expressing mock exasperation with the interviewer's question. Likewise, if I say, "They stole my fucking laptop!" the laptop need not have been execrable; it could have been a sleek titanium PowerBook with a 17-inch screen and a 1.67-gigahertz processor.[82] Expletives indicate that something is lamentable about an entire state of affairs, not the entity named by the noun, though properties of that entity may have something to do with why the state of affairs is lamentable. Just as important, the situation has to be lamentable from the point of view of the speaker, not of any of the characters mentioned in the sentence or discourse. If someone reports to you that *John says his landlord is a fucking scoutmaster,* you attribute the disrespect for scoutmasters to the speaker, not John, despite the fact that the *fucking* is inside the clause that conveys what John said.[83]

Part of the solution to this linguistic puzzle is that

expletives like *bloody* and *fucking* arose from the process by which one taboo word substitutes for another despite their having nothing else in common (the process that allowed *Where in hell* to beget *Where the fuck*, and *Holy Mary* to inspire *Holy shit*). With the expletives in *fucking scoutmaster* or *bloody empire*, the historical source is *damned* or *God-damned*, which persist today in expletives like *Damn Yankees, They stole my goddam laptop*, and *abso-goddam-lutely*. (*Damned* became *damn* when the insubstantial *-ed* got swallowed in pronunciation and overlooked in perception, as it did in *ice cream, mincemeat*, and *box set*, formerly *iced cream, minced meat*, and *boxed set*.) If something has been damned, it is condemnable, pitiable, and no longer of earthly use. One can imagine this connotation summoning words with similar emotional overtones like *fucking, bloody, dirty, lousy*, and *stupid*. They probably took their place alongside *damned* once religious expletives started to lose their sting in the history of English.

The other part of the solution is that affect-laden words can sometimes escape the usual grammatical machinery that computes who did what to whom from the arrangement of words in a parse tree. Linguists such as Christopher Potts argue that the grammar of English not only allows speakers to make an assertion in a sentence—what is "at issue"—but also provides them with ways to editorialize and comment on the assertion.[84] Sometimes called conventional implicatures, these devices allow a speaker to convey his attitude about what is being talked about, such as his opinion of the outcome or his degree of respect for one of the participants. One such device allows an attitude-laden word to break free of the actors in the drama being described and gravitate to the worldview of the speaker. For instance, if I say *Sue believes that that jerk Dave got promoted,* it's quite possible that Sue has a high opinion of Dave, but I am implying that I do not. This is just the scheme of interpretation that governs taboo expletives like *fucking* and *bloody.*

The swappability of taboo terms also explains the mystery of *Fuck you.* Woody Allen's joke about telling a driver to be fruitful and multiply but not in those words assumes that *Fuck you* is a second-person imperative, like *Get fucked* or *Fuck yourself.* Lenny Bruce made the same assumption, as did Bill Bryson in his delightful book *The Mother Tongue: English and How It Got That Way:*

> English is unusual in including the impossible and the pleasurable. It is a strange and little-noted idiosyncrasy of our tongue that when we wish to express extreme fury we entreat the object of our rage to undertake an anatomical impossibility, or, stranger still, to engage in the one activity that is bound to give him more pleasure than almost anything else. Can there be, when you think about it, a more improbable sentiment than "Get fucked"? We might as well snarl, "Make a lot of money" or "Have a nice day."[85]

But Quang makes short work of this theory.[86] For one thing, in a second-person imperative the pronoun has to be *yourself,* not *you*—Madonna's hit song was titled

"Express Yourself," not "Express You." For another, true imperatives like *Close the door* can be embedded in a number of other constructions:

> I said to close the door.
> Don't close the door.
> Go close the door.
> Close the door or I'll take away your cookies.
> Close the door and turn off the light.
> Close the door when you leave tonight.

But *Fuck you* cannot:

> *I said to fuck you.
> *Don't fuck you.
> *Go fuck you.
> *Fuck you or I'll take away your cookies.
> *Fuck you and turn off the light.
> *Fuck you when you leave tonight.

The difference can be seen with third-person objects as well, as in *Fuck communism!* Though you can conjoin two imperatives sharing an object, as in *Clean and press these pants*, you can't conjoin the imprecation with a true imperative, as in **Describe and fuck communism*.

Quang does not evaluate another folk etymology of *Fuck you*, namely that it's short for *I fuck you*. This is certainly compatible with the conceptual metaphor in which sex is a kind of exploitation or damage, but it makes no sense on linguistic grounds. The tense is wrong, the missing subject is unexplained, and there are no parallel constructions. Nor is there any historical evidence that *I fuck you* was ever a common curse in English.

The simplest explanation is that the *fuck* in *Fuck you* is like the *fuck* in *Where the fuck* and *a fucking scoutmaster:* a substitution for an older religious epithet with similar emotional force. In this case, the obvious source is *Damn you* (perhaps shortened from *God damn you* and *May God damn you*). The original semantics would have been a kind of third-person imperative meaning "May it be so," which is common in blessings ("May you be forever young") and curses (as in "May you live like a chandelier: hang by day and burn by night"). But the curse melted into a holistic pronouncement of disapproval. As Quang notes, *Fuck you* resembles not just *Damn you* but other constructions that express nothing but a strong attitude of the speaker toward the object: *To hell with you!, Shit on you!, Bless you!, Hooray for you!,* and the sarcastic *Bully for you!*

The remaining use of taboo language is cathartic—the blurting out of *damn, hell, shit, fuck,* or *bugger* in moments of sudden pain, frustration, or regret. If you ask people why they do it, they'll say that it "releases tension" or helps them "let off steam." This is the hydraulic metaphor for emotion, also seen in *venting one's feelings, finding an outlet, bottling up rage,* and *exploding with anger.* Though it undoubtedly captures what it feels like to express frustration, the hydraulic metaphor doesn't *explain* the feeling. Neuroscientists have not found vessels or pipes in the brain carrying heated fluid, just networks of neurons that fire in complex patterns. Nor is there a law of thermodynamics that could explain why the articulation of *Oh, fuck* would enable a dissipation of energy any more effectively than *Oh, my* or *Fiddle-dee-dee*.

The brain has other mechanisms, though, that may play a role in cathartic swearing. One of them is an electro-physiological response that kicks in when people notice they have just made an error.[87] It emanates from the anterior cingulate cortex, a part of the limbic system involved in the monitoring of cognitive conflict. In public, cognitive neuroscientists call this response the Error-Related Negativity; in private they call it the Oh-Shit Wave.

Also relevant are the limbic circuits in mammals that underlie the experience of anger. One of them, called the Rage circuit, runs from a part of the amygdala down through the hypothalamus (the tiny brain cluster that regulates motivation) and then into the gray matter of the midbrain.[88] The Rage circuit originally housed a reflex in which a suddenly wounded or confined animal would erupt in a furious struggle to startle, injure, and escape from a predator, often accompanied by a blood-curdling yowl. Anyone who has accidentally sat on a cat or stepped on the tail of a dog may discover a new sound in their pet's repertoire, sometimes followed by fresh clawmarks or teethmarks on their leg. The reaction has been studied in a long line of research in experimental psychology on an idea called the Frustration-Aggression hypothesis.[89] When two rats are put together in a chamber and given an electric shock, for example, they will start to fight. A rat will also attack another rat if a reward such as food is suddenly withdrawn, presumably an adaptation to the sudden theft of food, space, or other resources by a fellow animal. The underlying brain circuits have been conserved in human evolution. When this pathway is electrically stimulated in neurological patients during brain surgery, they experience a sudden intense rage.[90]

So here is a hypothesis about cathartic swearing. A sudden pain or frustration engages the Rage circuit, which activates parts of the limbic brain connected with negative emotion. Among them are representations of concepts with a strong emotional charge and the words connected to them, particularly the versions in the right hemisphere, with its heavier involvement in unpleasant emotions. The surge of an impulse for defensive violence may also remove the safety catches on aggressive acts ordinarily held in place by the basal ganglia, since discretion is not the better part of valor during what could be the last five seconds of your life. In humans, these inhibited responses may include the uttering of taboo words. Recall that the Rage response in animals also includes a fearsome yelp. Perhaps the combination of a firing up of negative concepts and words, a release of inhibition on antisocial acts, and the urge to make a sudden sharp noise culminates in an obscenity rather than the traditional mammalian shriek. (Of course, when people experience severe pain, they show that our species has also retained the ability to holler and howl.) Cathartic swearing, then, would come from a cross-wiring of the mammalian Rage circuit with human concepts and vocal routines.

The problem with the cross-wiring theory is that angry expletives are *conventional*. Like our other words and formulas, they depend on a memorized pairing between a sound and a meaning which is shared throughout a language community. When we bump our heads, we don't shout *Cunt!* or *Whore!* or *Prick!*, though these words are just as taboo as *shit, fuck,* and *damn* (and indeed are the translations of toe-stubbing cries in other languages). Also, the expletive is keyed to the cause of the misfortune. People shout *Asshole!* when they suffer a sudden affront from a human perpetrator, but not when they pick up a hot casserole or have a mousetrap snap on their finger. So the cathartic swear words are specific to the occasion and specific to the language. As Mrs. Pearce said of Eliza's use of the *b*-word, we learn them at our mother's knee, or perhaps more often at our father's. When I was four years old and sitting in the front seat of the car next to my father, the door swung open as we rounded a curve, and I said, "Oh, shit!," proud of knowing what an adult would say in those circumstances. I was quickly reprimanded in a show of hypocrisy that is one of the perquisites of parenthood.

Why should we go to the trouble of learning specific words for cathartic swearing rather than just letting our rage fire up any old taboo word? Cathartic swearing is part of a larger linguistic phenomenon called ejaculations or response cries.[91] Consider the following list:

aha, ah, aw, bah, bleh, boy, brrr, eek, eeuw, eh, goody, ha, hey, hmm, hmph, huh, mmm, my, oh, ohgod, omigod, ooh, oops, ouch, ow, oy, phew, pooh, shh, shoo, ugh, uh, uh-oh, um, whee, whoa, whoops, wow, yay, yes!, yikes, yipe, yuck

At first glance these seem less like real words than transliterations of the noises that escape from our mouths when we are in the throes of a strong feeling. They can't be used in a grammatical sentence (*I like goody; *I hate ouch*), and many of them violate the sound pattern of English (like *eeuw, hmph,* and *shh*). Nor are they spoken on cue when a speaker takes the floor in the give-and-take of a conversation.

But they really are words, with conventional sounds and meanings. The sounds are standardized, not just emitted as the feeling arises, to the point that many people articulate the spelling that cartoonists use to render people's exclamations onomatopoeically, like "Gulp!" "Tisk, tisk!" and "Phew!" And one of the most obvious giveaways that a speaker is foreign is the use of the wrong exclamation, as when an American interrupts his fluent French with the unmistakably Anglophone *um* or *ouch*. According to the joke, a Jewish woman trying to pass as a WASP at an exclusive country club wades into an ice-cold swimming pool. She shouts, "Oy vey! . . . whatever that means."

What *oy vey* and other response cries mean are as conventional as other words in a language. What do you say when you see an adorable baby? When you're cold? When you discover a worm in your apple? When you drop a napkin? When you discover the open window that's been letting in a draft? When you warm yourself with a spoonful of hot soup? Every English speaker knows which word to choose from the list.

The sociologist Erving Goffman was a theater critic of everyday life, analyzing the staging and dialogue that we use to manage the impression of a real or imagined audience.[92] One goal in this performance, he suggested, is to reassure onlookers that we are sane, competent, reasonable human beings, with transparent goals and intelligible responses to the current situation. Ordinarily this requires that we not talk to ourselves in public, but we make an exception when a sudden turn of events puts our rationality or effectiveness to the test. My favorite example is when we do an about-face in a hallway and mutter a soliloquy explaining to no one in particular that we forgot something in our office, as if to reassure any onlookers that we are not a lunatic who lurches around at random.

Goffman argues that there is a good reason we utter response cries: to signal our competence and shared understanding of the situation to a generic audience.[93] A person who knocks over a glass might be a klutz, but if he says *whoops*, then at least we know that he didn't intend the outcome and regrets that it happened. A person who says *yuck* after dripping pizza sauce on his shirt or stepping in dog feces is someone we understand better than someone who would seem not to care. And so it is with cathartic swearing. Faced with a sudden challenge to our goals or well-being, we inform the world that the setback matters to us, indeed, that it matters at an emotional level that calls up our worst thoughts and is at the boundaries of voluntary control.

Like other response cries, taboo outbursts are calibrated to the severity of the setback, *shoot* indicating a minor annoyance and *fuck* a more serious one. And depending on the choice of word and the tone in which it is uttered, an outburst can summon help, intimidate an adversary, or warn a careless actor of the harm he is inadvertently causing. Goffman sums up his theory: "Response cries, then, do not mark a flooding of emotion outward, but a flooding of relevance in."[94]

The Rage-circuit theory, which views cathartic swearing as a by-product, and the response-cry theory, which views it as an adaptation, are not mutually exclusive. Many ordinary response cries must have arisen as conventional renderings of vocal sounds, like *brr* for chattering teeth or *yuck* for expelling something from the back of the mouth. This ritualization may have shaped cathartic swearing as well. The epithets may have originated as Tourette-like outbursts of taboo words released by the Rage circuit and then were conventionalized into standard response cries for that kind of trespass or misfortune. Some cognitive neuroscientists have revived Darwin's suggestion that verbalized outbursts were the evolutionary missing link between primate calls and human languages.[95] If so, swearing would have played a more important role in the human career than most people would acknowledge.

Swearing, Con and Pro

So what should we do about profanity? Does the science of swearing cast any light on the controversies over shock jocks, clean airwaves, and broadcast decency? As far as policy is concerned, my remarks will be few and banal. It seems to me that free speech is the bedrock of democracy and that it is not among the legitimate functions of government to punish people who use certain words or allow others to use them. On the other hand, private media have the prerogative of enforcing a house style, driven by standards of taste and the demands of the market, that excludes words their audience doesn't enjoy hearing. In other words, if an entertainer says *fucking brilliant,* it's none of the government's business, but if some people would rather not explain to their young children what a blow job is, there should be television channels that don't force them to. Rather than review policy issues any more deeply than this, I hope to say a few words about how the psycholinguistics of taboo language might inform our judgment about when to discourage, when to tolerate, and even when to welcome profanity.

Language has often been called a weapon, and people should be mindful about where to aim it and when to fire. The common denominator of taboo words is the act of forcing a disagreeable thought on someone, and it's worth considering how often one really wants one's audience to be reminded of excrement, urine, and exploitative sex. Even in its mildest form, intended only to keep the listener's attention, the lazy use of profanity can feel like a series of jabs in the ribs. They are annoying to the listener, and a confession by the speaker that he can think of no other way to make his words worth attending to. It's all the more damning for writers, who have the luxury of choosing their words off-line from the half-million-word phantasmagoria of the English lexicon. A journalist who, in writing about the cruelty of an East German Stasi guard, can do no better than to call him a *fucker* needs to get a good thesaurus.[96]

Also calling for reflection is whether a linguistic taboo is always a bad thing. Why are we offended—why *should* we be offended—when an outsider refers to an African American as a *nigger,* or a woman as a *cunt,* or a Jewish person as *a fucking Jew*? The terms have no real meaning, so the offense cannot come from their perpetuating a stereotype or endorsing oppression. Nor is it a reaction to learning that the speaker harbors an abominable attitude. These days someone who displayed the same attitude by simply saying "I hate African Americans, women, and Jews" would be stigmatizing himself far more than his targets, and would quickly be written off as a loathsome kook. I suspect that our sense of offense comes from the nature of speech recognition and from what it means to understand the connotation of a word. If you're an English speaker, you can't hear the words *nigger* or *cunt* or *fucking* without calling to mind what they mean to an implicit community of speakers, including the emotions that cling to them. To hear *nigger* ✱ is to try on, however briefly, the thought that there is something contemptible about African Americans, and thus to be complicit in a community that standardized that judgment by putting it into a word. The same thing happens with other taboo imprecations: just hearing the words feels morally corrosive, so we consider them not just unpleasant to think but not to be thought at all—that

✱ I disagree, as the attempt to 'reclaim' the word 'nigger' by the black population has rendered it an epithet used for social satire by a generation of whites, rather than a contemptible slur of a race.

is, taboo. None of this means that the words should be banned, only that their effects on listeners should be understood and anticipated.

Also deserving of reflection is why previous generations of speakers bequeathed us a language that treats certain topics with circumspection and restraint. Recall that the lexical libertines of the 1960s believed that taboos on sexual language were pointless and even harmful. They argued that removing the stigma from sexuality would eliminate shame and ignorance and thereby reduce venereal disease, illegitimate births, and other hazards of sex. But on this matter Saint Lenny turned out to be mistaken. Sexual language has become far more common since the early 1960s, but so have illegitimacy, sexually transmitted infections, rape, and the fallout of sexual competition, like anorexia in girls and swagger culture in boys. Though no one can pin down cause and effect, the changes are of a piece with the weakening of the fear and awe that used to surround thoughts about sex and that charged sexual language with taboo.

Those are some of the reasons to think twice about giving carte blanche to swearing. But there is another reason. If an overuse of taboo words, whether by design or laziness, blunts their emotional edge, it will have deprived us of a linguistic instrument that we sometimes sorely need. And this brings me to the arguments on the pro-swearing side.

To begin with, it's a fact of life that people swear. The responsibility of writers is to give a "just and lively image of human nature," and that includes portraying a character's language realistically when their art calls for it. When Norman Mailer wrote his true-to-life novel about World War II, *The Naked and the Dead,* in 1948, he knew it would be a betrayal of his depiction of the soldiers to have them speak without swearing. His compromise with the sensibilities of the day was to have them use the pseudo-epithet *fug.* (When Dorothy Parker met him she said, "So you're the man who doesn't know how to spell *fuck.*") Sadly, this prissiness is not a thing of the past. Some public television stations today are afraid to broadcast Martin Scorsese's documentary on the history of the blues and Ken Burns's documentary on World War II because of the salty language in their interviews with musicians and soldiers. The prohibition against swearing in broadcast media makes artists and historians into liars, and subverts the responsibility of grown-ups to learn how life is lived in worlds distant from their own.

Even when their characters are not soldiers, writers must sometimes let them swear in order to render human passion compellingly. In the film adaptation of Isaac Bashevis Singer's *Enemies: A Love Story,* a sweet Polish peasant girl has hidden a Jewish man in a hayloft during the Nazi occupation and becomes his doting wife when the war is over. When she confronts him over an affair he has been having, he loses control and slaps her in the face. Fighting back tears of rage, she looks him in the eye and says slowly, "I saved your life. I took the last bite of food out of my mouth and gave it to you in the hayloft. I carried out your *shit!*" No other word could convey the depth of her fury at his ingratitude.

For language lovers, the joys of swearing are not confined to the works of famous writers. Every idiom must have been the brainchild of some creative speaker lost in the mists of time, and many of the profane ones deserve our admiration. We should pause to applaud the poetic genius who gave us the soldiers' term for chipped beef on toast, *shit on a shingle,* and the male-to-male advisory for discretion in sexual matters, *Keep your pecker in your pocket.* Hats off, too, to the word-smiths who thought up the indispensable *pissing contest, crock of shit, pussy-whipped,* and *horse's ass,* not to mention that fine descriptor of the clueless, *He doesn't know shit from Shinola.* Among those in the historical record, Lyndon Johnson had a certain way with words when it came to summing up the people he distrusted, including a Kennedy aide ("He wouldn't know how to pour piss out of a boot if the instructions were printed on the heel"), Gerald Ford ("He can't fart and chew gum at the same time"), and J. Edgar Hoover ("I'd rather have him inside the tent pissing out than outside pissing in").

Profanity can be used effectively in poetry, such as in Philip Larkin's "This Be the Verse," his 1974 poem on how "man hands on misery to man":

> They fuck you up, your mum and dad.
> They may not mean to, but they do.
> They fill you with the faults they had
> And add some extra, just for you.[97]

And it can be used in scientific argumentation, as in

Judith Rich Harris's case against the belief that parents shape their children's characters:

> Poor old Mum and Dad: publicly accused by their son, the poet, and never given a chance to reply to his charges. They shall have one now, if I may take the liberty of speaking for them:
>
> > How sharper than a serpent's tooth
> > To hear your child make such a fuss.
> > It isn't fair—it's not the truth—
> > He's fucked up, yes, but not by us.[98]

It can be even used in a protest against government sanctions on profanity, as in "The FCC Song" by Monty Python's Eric Idle:

> Fuck you very much, the FCC.
> Fuck you very much for fining me.
> Five thousand bucks a fuck,
> So I'm really out of luck.
> That's more than Heidi Fleiss was charging me.

Which is also the clearest illustration I know of the logician's distinction between the "mention" and "use" of words.

When used judiciously, swearing can be hilarious, poignant, and uncannily descriptive. More than any other form of language, it recruits our expressive faculties to the fullest: the combinatorial power of syntax; the evocativeness of metaphor; the pleasure of alliteration, meter, and rhyme; and the emotional charge of our attitudes, both thinkable and unthinkable. It engages the full expanse of the brain: left and right, high and low, ancient and modern. Shakespeare, no stranger to earthy imprecations himself, had Caliban speak for the entire human race when he said, "You taught me language, and my profit on't is, I know how to curse."

Notes

1. Allan & Burridge, 1991; Dooling, 1996; Hughes, 1991/1998; Jay, 2000; Wajnryb, 2005.
2. Bruce, 1965/1991.
3. Kennedy, 2002.
4. Denfeld, 1995; Dooling, 1996; Patai, 1998; Saporta, 1994.
5. Allan & Burridge, 1991; Jay, 2000; Wajnryb, 2005.
6. Allan & Burridge, 1991; Jay, 2000; Wajnryb, 2005.
7. Hughes, 1991/1998.
8. Hughes, 1991/1998, p. 3.
9. From the CD accompanying Collins & Skover, 2002.
10. Hughes, 1991/1998.
11. Allan & Burridge, 1991; Jay, 2000; Wajnryb, 2005.
12. Hughes, 1991/1998.
13. Allan & Burridge, 1991; Aman, 1987; Crystal, 1997; Jay, 2000; Wajnryb, 2005.
14. Wajnryb, 2005, p. 223.
15. Aman, 1987; Solt, 1987.
16. Allan & Burridge, 1991; Rosenblum & Pinker, 1983.
17. Osgood, Suci, & Tannenbaum, 1957.
18. Beeman, 2005.
19. LeDoux, 1996; Panksepp, 1998.
20. Isenberg et al., 1999; LaBar & Phelps, 1998; Lewis et al., in press.
21. Harris, Gleason, & Aycicegi, 2006; Jay, 2000; Matthew, Richards, & Eysenck, 1989.
22. Harris, Gleason, & Aycicegi, 2006.
23. Roelofs, in press.
24. MacKay et al., 2004.
25. Allan & Burridge, 1991; Hughes, 1991/1998.
26. S. Pinker, "Racist Language, Real and Imagined," *New York Times*, February 2, 1999.
27. Dronkers, Pinker, & Damasio, 1999.
28. Jay, 2000; Van Lancker & Cummings, 1999.
29. Van Lancker & Cummings, 1999.
30. Jay, 2000; Van Lancker & Cummings, 1999; Van Lancker & Sidtis, 2006.
31. Dronkers, Pinker, & Damasio, 1999; Pinker, 1997a; Pinker, 1999.

32. Etcoff, 1986.
33. Wise, Murray, & Gerfen, 1996.
34. Ullman et al., 1997.
35. Speedie, Wertman, & Heilman, 1993.
36. Singer, 2005.
37. Jay, 2000; Van Lancker & Cummings, 1999.
38. Van Lancker & Cummings, 1999.
39. Wegner, 1989.
40. Allan & Burridge, 1991; Hughes, 1991/1998.
41. Kiparsky, 1973.
42. Pinker, 1994b; Pinker, 1999.
43. Allan & Burridge, 1991; Crystal, 2003.
44. Hughes, 1991/1998, pp. 22–23.
45. Allan & Burridge, 1991; Hughes, 1991/1998.
46. Frank, 1988; Pinker, 1997b, chap. 6; Schelling, 1960.
47. Hughes, 1991/1998.
48. Allan & Burridge, 1991; Hughes, 1991/1998.
49. Pinker, 2002, chap. 15; Tetlock et al., 2000.
50. Hughes, 1991/1998, p. 12.
51. Hughes, 1991/1998.
52. Allan & Burridge, 1991.
53. Curtis & Biran, 2001, p. 21.
54. Allan & Burridge, 1991; Harris, 1989; Rozin & Fallon, 1987.
55. Rozin & Fallon, 1987.
56. Quoted by Curtis & Biran, 2001.
57. Curtis & Biran, 2001. See also Rozin & Fallon, 1987, and Pinker, 1997b, chap. 6.
58. Rozin & Fallon, 1987.
59. Curtis & Biran, 2001; Rozin & Fallon, 1987.
60. From the biographical movie *Lenny*.
61. Buss, 1994; Symons, 1979.
62. Buss, 1994; Symons, 1979.
63. Jay, 2000; Van Lancker & Cummings, 1999; Wajnryb, 2005.
64. Denfeld, 1995; Dooling, 1996; Patai, 1998.
65. Dworkin, 1979, p. 133; cited in Denfeld, 1995, p. 23.
66. Allan & Burridge, 1991.
67. Quoted in Hughes, 1991/1998.
68. Hughes, 1991/1998, p. 122.
69. Allan & Burridge, 1991; Aman, 1987.
70. Quoted in Wajnryb, 2005, p. 48.

71. Levin, 1985; Levin, 1993; Pinker, 1989.
72. The following examples are marginally acceptable to me (in their grammar, if not their practice): *Clarence fucked at the goat for three minutes but was interrupted by Old MacDonald* (conative); *He fucked her in the armpit / He fucked her armpit* (possessor-raising); *Goats fuck easily* (middle). The following are not: *John fucked a dildo into the goat* (contact locative; compare *John fucked the goat with a dildo,* which is fine); *At three o'clock, the goat fucked* (anticausative).
73. Quang Fuc Dong, 1971/1992b.
74. Sheidlower, 1995.
75. Zwicky et al., 1971/1992.
76. J. S. Farmer & W. E. Henley, *Slang and Its Analogues,* 1890–1904, quoted in Hughes, 1991/1998, p. 271.
77. Quang Fuc Dong, 1971/1992a.
78. Nunberg, 2004. Some adjectives, like *former* and *alleged,* also fail these tests, but they differ from *fucking* in other ways.
79. Shad, 1971/1992.
80. Nunberg, 2004.
81. The interview continues:
    INTERVIEWER: Who's your favorite Charlie's Angel?
    CLEESE: Noam Chomsky.
82. Thanks to Geoffrey Pullum for the laptop example.
83. Quang Fuc Dong, 1971/1992a; Potts, 2005.
84. Potts, 2005.
85. Bryson, 1990, p. 211.
86. Quang Fuc Dong, 1971/1992a.
87. Yeung, Botvinick, & Cohen, 2004.
88. Panksepp, 1998.
89. Dollard et al., 1939; Panksepp, 1998.
90. Panksepp, 1998.
91. Goffman, 1978.
92. Goffman, 1959.
93. Goffman, 1978.
94. Goffman, 1978, p. 814.
95. Code, in press; Darwin, 1874; Wray, 1998.
96. From a book review in a recent issue of a respected opinion magazine.
97. Larkin, 2003.
98. Harris, 1998, p. 350.

References

Allan, K., & Burridge, K. 1991. *Euphemism and dysphemism: Language used as shield and weapon.* New York: Oxford University Press.

Aman, R. 1987. *The best of Maledicta: The International Journal of Verbal Aggression.* Philadelphia: Running Press.

Beeman, J.-J. 2005. Bilateral brain processes for comprehending natural language. *Trends in Cognitive Science, 9,* 512–518.

Bruce, L. 1965/1991. *How to talk dirty and influence people: An autobiography.* New York: Simon & Schuster.

Bryson, B. 1990. *The mother tongue: English and how it got that way.* New York: Morrow.

Buss, D. M. 1994. *The evolution of desire.* New York: Basic Books.

Code, C. In press. First in, last out? The evolution of aphasic lexical speech automatisms to agrammatism and the evolution of human communication. *Interaction Studies.*

Collins, R. K. L., & Skover, D. M. 2002. *The trials of Lenny Bruce: The fall and rise of an American icon.* Naperville, Ill.: Sourcebooks.

Crystal, D. 1997. *The Cambridge Encyclopedia of Language* (2nd ed.). New York: Cambridge University Press.

Crystal, D. 2003. *The Cambridge Encyclopedia of the English Language* (2nd ed.). New York: Cambridge University Press.

Curtis, V., & Biran, A. 2001. Dirt, disgust, and disease: Is hygiene in our genes? *Perspectives in Biology and Medicine, 44,* 17–31.

Darwin, C. 1874. *The descent of man, and selection in relation to sex* (2nd ed.). New York: Hurst & Company.

Denfeld, R. 1995. *The new Victorians: A young woman's challenge to the old feminist order.* New York: Warner Books.

Dollard, J., Miller, N. E., Doob, L. W., Mowrer, O. H., & Sears, R. R. 1939. *Frustration and aggression.* New Haven, Conn.: Yale University Press.

Dooling, R. 1996. *Blue streak: Swearing, free speech, and sexual harassment.* New York: Random House.

Dronkers, N., Pinker, S., & Damasio, A. R. 1999. Language and the aphasias. In E. R. Kandel, J. H. Schwartz, & T. M. Jessell (Eds.), *Principles of neural science* (4th ed.). Norwalk, Conn.: Appleton & Lange.

Etcoff, N. L. 1986. The neuropsychology of emotional expression. In G. Goldstein & R. E. Tarter (Eds.), *Advances in clinical neuropsychology* (Vol. 3). New York: Plenum.

81

References

Frank, R. H. 1988. *Passions within reason: The strategic role of the emotions*. New York: Norton.

Goffman, E. 1959. *The presentation of self in everyday life*. New York: Doubleday.

Goffman, E. 1978. Response cries. *Language, 54*, 787–815.

Harris, C. L., Gleason, J. B., & Aycicegi, A. 2006. When is a first language more emotional? Psychophysiological evidence from bilingual speakers. In A. Pavlenko (Ed.), *Bilingual minds: Emotional experience, expression, and representation*. Clevedon, U.K.: Multilingual Matters.

Harris, J. R. 1989. *Our kind: The evolution of human life and culture*. New York: HarperCollins.

Harris, J. R. 1998. *The nurture assumption: Why children turn out the way they do*. New York: Free Press.

Hughes, G. 1991/1998. *Swearing: A social history of foul language, oaths, and profanity in English*. New York: Penguin.

Isenberg, N., Silbersweig, D., Engelien, A., Emmerich, K., Malavade, K., Beati, B., et al. 1999. Linguistic threat activates the human amygdala. *Proceedings of the National Academy of Sciences, 96*, 10456–10459.

Jay, T. 2000. *Why we curse: A neuro-psycho-social theory of speech*. Philadelphia: John Benjamins.

Kennedy, R. 2002. *Nigger: The strange career of a troublesome word*. New York: Pantheon.

Kiparsky, P. 1973. The role of linguistics in a theory of poetry. *Daedalus, 102*, 231–244.

LaBar, K. S., & Phelps, E. A. 1998. Arousal-mediated memory consolidation: Role of the medial temporal lobe in humans. *Psychological Science, 9*, 490–493.

Larkin, P. 2003. *Collected poems* (A. Thwaite, Ed.). London: Faber & Faber.

LeDoux, J. E. 1996. *The emotional brain: The mysterious underpinnings of emotional life*. New York: Simon & Schuster.

Levin, B. 1985. *Lexical semantics in review: An introduction* (Lexicon Project Working Paper #1). Cambridge, Mass.: MIT Center for Cognitive Science.

Levin, B. 1993. *English verb classes and alternations: A preliminary investigation*. Chicago: University of Chicago Press.

Lewis, P. A., Critchley, H. D., Rothstein, P., & Dolan, R. J. In press. Neural correlates of processing valence and arousal in affective words. *Cerebral Cortex*.

MacKay, D. G., Shafto, M., Taylor, J. K., Marian, D. E., Abrams, L., & Dyer, J. R. 2004. Relations between emotion, memory, and attention:

References

Evidence from taboo Stroop, lexical decision, and immediate memory tasks. *Memory & Cognition, 32,* 474–488.

Matthew, A., Richards, A., & Eysenck, M. 1989. Interpretation of homophones related to threat in anxiety states. *Journal of Abnormal Psychology, 98,* 31–34.

Nunberg, G. 2004. Imprecisional categories. *The Language Log.* http://itre.cis.upenn.edu/~mgl/languagelog/archives/000614.html..

Osgood, C. E., Suci, G., & Tannenbaum, P. 1957. *The measurement of meaning.* Urbana, Ill.: University of Illinois Press.

Panksepp, J. 1998. *Affective neuroscience: The foundations of human and animal emotions.* New York: Oxford University Press.

Patai, D. 1998. *Heterophobia: Sexual harassment and the future of feminism.* New York: Rowman & Littlefield.

Pinker, S. 1989. *Learnability and cognition: The acquisition of argument structure.* Cambridge, Mass.: MIT Press.

Pinker, S. 1994a. How could a child use verb syntax to learn verb semantics? *Lingua, 92,* 377–410.

Pinker, S. 1994b. *The Language Instinct.* New York: HarperCollins.

Pinker, S. 1997a. Words and rules in the human brain. *Nature, 387,* 547–548.

Pinker, S. 1997b. *How the mind works.* New York: Norton.

Pinker, S. 1999. *Words and rules: The ingredients of language.* New York: HarperCollins.

Pinker, S. 2002. *The blank slate: The modern denial of human nature.* New York: Viking.

Potts, C. 2005. *The logic of conventional implicatures.* New York: Oxford University Press.

Quang Fuc Dong. 1971/1992b. A note on conjoined noun phrases. In A. M. Zwicky, P. H. Salus, R. I. Binnick, & A. L. Vanek (Eds.), *Studies out in left field: Defamatory essays presented to James D. McCawley on the occasion of his 33rd or 34th birthday.* Philadelphia: John Benjamins.

Roelofs, A. In press. The visual-auditory color-word Stroop asymmetry and its time course. *Memory & Cognition.*

Rosenblum, T., & Pinker, S. 1983. Word magic revisited: Monolingual and bilingual pre-schoolers' understanding of the word-object relationships. *Child Development, 54,* 773–780.

Rozin, P., & Fallon, A. 1987. A perspective on disgust. *Psychological Review, 94,* 23–41.

Saporta, S. 1994. *Society, language, and the university.* New York: Vantage.

Schelling, T. C. 1960. *The strategy of conflict.* Cambridge, Mass.: Harvard University Press.

References

Shad, U. P., 1971/1992. Some unnatural habits. In A. M. Zwicky, P. H. Salus, R. I. Binnick, & A. L. Vanek (Eds.), *Studies out in left field: Defamatory essays presented to James D. McCawley on the occasion of of his 33rd or 34th birthday*. Philadelphia: John Benjamins.

Sheidlower, J. 1995. *The F-word*. New York: Random House.

Singer, H. S. 2005. Tourette syndrome: From behavior to biology. *Lancet Neurology, 4*, 149–159.

Solt, J. 1987. Japanese sexual maledicta. In R. Aman (Ed.), *The best of Maledicta: The International Journal of Verbal Aggression*. Philadelphia: Running Press.

Speedie, L. J., Wertman, J. T., & Heilman, K. M. 1993. Disruption of automatic speech following a right basal ganglia lesion. *Neurology, 43*, 1768–1774.

Symons, D. 1979. *The evolution of human sexuality*. New York: Oxford University Press.

Tetlock, P. E., Kristel, O. V., Elson, B., Freen, M. C., & Lerner, J. 2000. The psychology of the unthinkable: Taboo trade offs:, forbidden base rates, and heretical counterfactuals. *Journal of Personality and Social Psychology, 78*, 853–870.

Ullman, M. T., Corkin, S., Coppola, M., Hickok, G., Growdon, J. H., Koroshetz, W. J., & Pinker, S. 1997. A neural dissociation within language: Evidence that the mental dictionary is part of declarative memory, and that grammatical rules are processed by the procedural system. *Journal of Cognitive Neuroscience, 9*, 289–299.

Van Lancker, D., & Cummings, J. L. 1999. Expletives: Neurolinguistic and neurobehavioral perspectives on swearing. *Brain Research Reviews, 31*, 83–104.

Van Lancker, D., & Sidtis, B. 2006. Formulaic expressions in spontaneous speech of left- and right-hemisphere-damaged subjects. *Aphasiology, 20*, 411–426.

Wajnryb, R. 2005. *Expletive deleted: A good look at bad language*. New York: Random House.

Wegner, D. 1989. *White bears and other unwanted thoughts: Suppression, obsession, and the psychology of mental control*. New York: Guilford.

Wise, S., Murray, E., & Gerfen, C. 1996. The frontal cortex-basal ganglia system in primates. *Critical Reviews in Neurobiology 10*, 317–356.

Wray, A. 1998. Protolanguage as a holistic system for social interaction. *Language and Communication, 18*, 47–67.

Yeung, N., Botvinick, M. M., & Cohen, J. D. 2004. The neural basis of error detection: Conflict monitoring and the Error-Related Negativity. *Psychological Review, 11*, 931–959.

References

Zwicky, A. M., Salus, P. H., Binnick, R. I., & Vanek, A. L. (Eds.). 1971/1992. *Studies out in left field: Defamatory essays presented to James D. McCawley on the occasion of his 33rd or 34th birthday.* Philadelphia: John Benjamins.

PENGUIN SCIENCE

THE BLANK SLATE STEVEN PINKER

'The best book on human nature that I or anyone else will ever read. Truly magnificent' Matt Ridley, *Sunday Telegraph*

'A passionate defence of the enduring power of human nature ... both life-affirming and deeply satisfying' Tim Lott, *Daily Telegraph*

'Brilliant ... enjoyable, informative, clear, humane' *New Scientist*

'If you think the nature/nurture debate has been resolved, you are wrong. It is about to be reignited with a vengeance ... this book is required reading' *Literary Review*

'Startling ... Pinker makes his main argument persuasively and with great verve ... This is a breath of air for a topic that has been politicized for too long' *Economist*

HOW THE MIND WORKS STEVEN PINKER

'Why do memories fade? Why do we lose our tempers? Why do fools fall in love? Pinker's objective in this erudite account is to explore the nature and history of the human mind' *Sunday Times*

'Witty popular science that you enjoy reading for the writing as well as for the science' *The New York Review of Books*

THE LANGUAGE INSTINCT STEVEN PINKER

'A marvellously readable book...illuminates every facet of human language: its biological origin, its uniqueness to humanity, its acquisition by children, its grammatical structure, the production and perception of speech, the pathology of language disorders and its unstoppable evolution' *Nature*

'An extremely valuable book, informative and well written' Noam Chomsky

'Brilliant ... Pinker describes every aspect of language, from the resolution of ambiguity to the way speech evolved ... he expounds difficult ideas with clarity, wit and polish' Stuart Sutherland, *Observer*

PENGUIN PSYCHOLOGY

BLINK
THE POWER OF THINKING WITHOUT THINKING
MALCOLM GLADWELL

'Astonishing … *Blink* really does make you rethink the way you think' *Daily Mail*

'Trust my snap judgement, buy this book: you'll be delighted' *The New York Times*

An art expert sees a ten-million-dollar sculpture and instantly spots it's a fake.
A marriage analyst knows within minutes whether a couple will stay together. A
fire-fighter suddenly senses he has to get out of a blazing building. A speed dater
clicks with the right person …

This book is all about those moments when we 'know' something without
knowing why. Here Malcolm Gladwell, one of the world's most original thinkers,
explores the phenomenon of 'blink', showing how a snap judgement can be far
more effective than a cautious decision. By trusting your instincts, he reveals,
you'll never think about thinking in the same way again …

'Compelling, fiendishly clever' *Evening Standard*

'Brilliant … the implications for business, let alone love, are vast' *Observer*

'Superb … this wonderful book should be compulsory reading' *New Statesman*

'*Blink* might just change your life' *Esquire*

'Should you buy this book? You already know the answer to that'
Independent on Sunday

PENGUIN REFERENCE

THE MEANING OF TINGO
ADAM JACOT DE BOINOD

Did you know that the Albanians have twenty-seven words for moustache?

Or that in Hungary pigs go röf-röf-röf?

Or that tingo is an Easter Island word meaning 'to borrow things from a friend's house one by one until there's nothing left'?

Here are the most weird and wonderful words from all around the world, showing the curious ways different countries talk about food, emotions, animals and even facial hair – as well as many things you hadn't even realized had words to describe them …

'A book no well-stocked bookshelf, cistern-top or handbag should be without'
Stephen Fry

'A luscious list of linguistic one-liners' *Daily Express*

Penguin Psychology

TALKING OF LOVE
BORIS CYRULNIK

'This is a beautiful book, and a groundbreaking psychological work – almost a map for survival' *Daily Telegraph*

All of us suffer from trauma in our lives, whether it is a difficult childhood, the end of a love affair or a violent experience. Yet we need not be controlled by our pain. This groundbreaking work on the healing power of resilience shows us how it is possible for us to grow in the face of our problems and live again.

Psychoanalyst Boris Cyrulnik, himself a survivor of great trauma, has worked with victims of cruelty and disaster all over the world. Here he draws on a mixture of case histories, parables and personal recollections to explain how – at any stage of life, from adolescence to having children ourselves – it is possible to break free from trauma and use our pain to remake our destiny.

Talking of Love shows how, by translating trauma into words, life stories can be rewritten.

'Cyrulnik has healed people, and countries … it is rare to find an analyst who can convey his message without psychobabble. Cyrulnik's book is straightforward and, at times, humorous' *The Times*

'Cyrulnik provides us with the power of hope … a soothing and cathartic book' *New Statesman*

PENGUIN SCIENCE

MADNESS EXPLAINED
RICHARD BENTALL

Winner of the British Psychological Society Book Award 2004

'A radical new look at madness ... This is a book to seduce a new generation into psychiatry and psychology' *Independent*

'Full of insight and humanity' *Sunday TImes*

'A monumental new study ... brave, well-researched and accessible'
Scotland on Sunday

'Bentall demystifies psychosis and restores the patient to a proper place with the rest of humankind' Aaron T. Beck

SO SHALL WE REAP
COLIN TUDGE

'Dazzling ... humane ... important ... this book is a wake-up call'
Felicity Lawrence, *Guardian*

'Anyone who understands that the politics of food production is at least as important for the future of the planet as the politics of war or of business will want to read this excellent book' Hugh Fearnley-Whittingstall

'Masterful ... *Fast Food Nation* shed light on junk food. Tudge goes further, showing how junk politics have turned the adage "agriculture is just a business like any other" into a pernicious new global orthodoxy' *The Herald*

'Everyone concerned for the longer-term future of humanity should read this'
The Times Literary Supplement

He just wanted a decent book to read ...

Not too much to ask, is it? It was in 1935 when Allen Lane, Managing Director of Bodley Head Publishers, stood on a platform at Exeter railway station looking for something good to read on his journey back to London. His choice was limited to popular magazines and poor-quality paperbacks – the same choice faced every day by the vast majority of readers, few of whom could afford hardbacks. Lane's disappointment and subsequent anger at the range of books generally available led him to found a company – and change the world.

'We believed in the existence in this country of a vast reading public for intelligent books at a low price, and staked everything on it'
Sir Allen Lane, 1902–1970, founder of Penguin Books

The quality paperback had arrived – and not just in bookshops. Lane was adamant that his Penguins should appear in chain stores and tobacconists, and should cost no more than a packet of cigarettes.

Reading habits (and cigarette prices) have changed since 1935, but Penguin still believes in publishing the best books for everybody to enjoy. We still believe that good design costs no more than bad design, and we still believe that quality books published passionately and responsibly make the world a better place.

So wherever you see the little bird – whether it's on a piece of prize-winning literary fiction or a celebrity autobiography, political tour de force or historical masterpiece, a serial-killer thriller, reference book, world classic or a piece of pure escapism – you can bet that it represents the very best that the genre has to offer.

Whatever you like to read – trust Penguin.